Old and Cold

Orientation 101

Janice Saunders

Hamilton Books

A member of
Rowman & Littlefield
Lanham • Boulder • New York • Toronto • Plymouth, UK

Copyright © 2014 by Hamilton Books
4501 Forbes Boulevard, Suite 200, Lanham, Maryland 20706
Hamilton Books Aquisitions Department (301) 459-3366

10 Thornbury Road, Plymouth PL6 7PP, United Kingdom

All rights reserved

British Library Cataloguing in Publication Information Available

Library of Congress Control Number: 2013947448
ISBN: 978-0-7618-6220-8 (paper : paper)—ISBN: 978-0-7618-6221-5 (electronic)

Cover photograph by Jay Saunders.

To Ford and Joey
who are new

Contents

Preface ... vii

Acknowledgments ... xi

1 Hot Flashes and Cold Feet ... 1
2 "No, I'm not retarded; I just can't hear and I don't remember." ... 5
3 Preening ... 13
4 OMG! TARSU IMHO ... 23
5 Sex ... 31
6 Milk? When There's Wine? ... 39
7 Club Sandwich Generation ... 45
8 Avoid Stepping in the Fountain of Youth ... 51
9 The Funeral File ... 57
10 I Don't Know the Difference between Goldfish Food and a Puppy ... 63
11 Retired and Outrageous ... 69
12 New Tricks ... 75

Epilogue ... 83

Preface

I squandered my youth agonizing over the inevitability of aging and death (I won't bore you with the details of this irony). You can imagine, then, with what enthusiasm I read *Passages* by Gail Sheehy when it came out in 1976. Although far from senior status in the seventies, I wanted answers for anticipatory socialization into aging; I wanted to prepare for what lay ahead. I thought surely the book would prove helpful, if not therapeutic, and true to the hype, the author's descriptions of crises in different stages of adult life were insightful. Problem was, Sheehy's discourse concluded with a chapter on 50 year olds. Needless to say, she left my neurotic self disconsolate as I wondered, is there no life after 50?! In all fairness to Sheehy, she went on to address advancing years in *New Passages,* 1996, and *Passages,* 2006.

Now way over the proverbial hill, I no longer anticipate the vicissitudes of aging—I'm living them! I'm a retired professor who sorely misses the college classroom and my student groupies. I no longer teach history, I *am* history! In my profession I was in control, knowledgeable, up-to-date on the latest research in my field. I routinely related to sharp-minded colleagues, both young and not-so-young. I was "on top of it." Nowadays I pray to sustain only mild dementia.

I've put several decades, countless books, lots of study, and much life experience behind me since those days of acute anxiety about growing old. A whole new universe has opened up to me. I'm learning what it means to be counted among the "nearly elderly" (a recent gerontology concept referring to people roughly between 65 and 75 years of age), how age affects family and friends, and how to face a challenging, but still exciting, lifestyle. At present, my two children are almost middle-aged, I'm getting closer to my fiftieth wedding anniversary, and I'm in the process of downsizing our rambling family home and overgrown yard. As a grandmother, I strain physically to keep up with my young grandchildren whom I adore. Despite a few worn-out-body issues though, I'm having a delightful time. Life *is* good, as the clothing line proclaims.

This book is written for all those older as well as younger people who, like me, are curious to know about the perceptions and experiences of relatively "normal" folks my age (notice that I use the word "relatively" and that I bracket the word "normal" with quotation marks). While I hope that readers enjoy what I've written, I also hope to fill at least a little of the dearth of information on growing old. Aging, as in any stage of life, presents a plethora of concerns. It's infinitely easier to face the future if one has some inkling of what to expect.

Old and Cold is *not* a medical guide. Nor does it offer instructions on how to muddle your way through Medicare options or how to live with Alzheimer's (an oxymoronic phrase if ever I've seen one). Hopefully what you will find in these pages are sprinkles of wisdom, from those much more discerning and poetic than I, as well as humorous episodes. This is not one of those inane joke books that promote ageism. I'm not referring to those fun publications such as Hallmark's *Maxine*; I enjoy the heck out of Maxine's independent, feisty, take-no-prisoners attitude. I'm talking about the type of "literature" invariably found in tacky gift shops—you know the kind I mean.

If you discover whining as you read, not to worry; it's intended to be tongue-in-cheek or droll. You will rarely find the author maudlin about growing old. The worse you may discern is female chauvinism, but give me a break; there are plenty of books on the market about aging which are written by men from a male perspective. For you fellows, at least I've tried to adopt an egalitarian approach. If I haven't succeeded in doing so, I apologize up front to you and to Mikey, my beloved husband and constant helpmate on this project and innumerable other endeavors.

Herein lies a thoroughly candid, "real people" or "every man/woman" look at life in the years after vigorous youth but before decrepitude.

To borrow an analogy from Hemingway, life is a moveable feast. My peers and I progress towards the last course, or as I prefer to think of it, a sweet-sour dessert, topped off with an after dinner liquor.

I'm extremely grateful to the many folks, especially to Jennifer Rosti, who helped me with this manuscript. Jennifer provides steadfast, invaluable editorial expertise, exceptional insight, and delightful companionship in the process. Among her many skills, Jenny serves up a mean glass of southern style iced tea. I very much appreciate also the editorial comments and advice of literati Dr. Bobbye Au, Ruth Frazier, and Bill Beasley. My dear friend, Jenny Bradley, saved me untold hours of frustration with her technological aid. Many thanks as always to my cherished, multi-talented offspring, Jay and Jamie. Jamie labored through the final editing process with me and Jay designed the book cover, the second one he's done for me! Last, but not at all least, I give profuse thanks to my friends, whose stories I share along with mine.

Of course I alone bear responsibility for any errors that may occur herein.

Acknowledgments

Grateful acknowledgment is made for permission to reprint from the following: *The Sea* by John Banville (Vintage Books, copyright 2005); *Old Possum's Book of Practical Cats* (Faber and Faber Ltd., London, and Houghton Mifflin Harcourt Publishing Company, copyright 1939 by T.S. Eliot and renewed 1967 by Esme Valerie Eliot. All rights reserved) for excerpt from "Macavity: The Mystery Cat" by T.S. Eliot; *When I am an Old Woman I Shall Wear Purple* (Papier-Mache Press, copyright 1987, editor Sandra Martz) for "The Coming of Winter" by Shirley Vogler Meister; *Parade Magazine* for "Ask Marilyn," copyright April 2, 2000, by Marilyn vos Savant, all rights reserved; *Virginia Tech Research* (Virginia Tech Press, copyright 2011) for "Advice for making friends and keeping friends—don't use the 'O' word" by Susan Trulove; excerpts from "And Now You Want to Know if There is Anything Good to Say About Getting Older" which appears in *Forever Fifty and Other Negotiations* by Judith Viorst (published by Simon and Schuster, Inc. Copyright © 1989 by Judith Viorst. This usage granted by permission of The Choate Agency, LLC); and "Song of Myself," verse 52, by Walt Whitman (Dover Thrift Editions Series, copyright 1900 – present).

Chapter One

Hot Flashes and Cold Feet

>...We acquiesce to freezing winds and test
>our mettle 'gainst the spectral storms ahead,
>for there are forces that we can't arrest
>and states of nature that we need not dread.
>Beyond the winds lie gentler joys and peace
>that sanctify our fate and death's caprice...
>—from "The Coming of Winter" by Shirley Vogler Meister

Seeking reprieve from the recent bitterly cold Virginia winter, some female pals and I traveled south for a beach weekend. En route one of my friends in the backseat yelped, "Turn on the A-C. I'm dying back here!" She was having a hot flash. Continuing hot flashes at our age—some of us will never see seventy again—is maddening! At night we throw bed covers off and on, off and on. How long does this annoying heat, often followed by a bone-deep chill, go on?

One tribulation of aging I've discovered is that the body no longer adjusts well to temperature extremes. Reminiscent of Goldilocks' porridge, I'm either too hot or too cold, seldom just right.

During the winter, we seniors contrive various tactics to keep our bodies toasty. One of my dear cohorts suffered from the severe cold last winter much more than I. She lamented that the two worse times of the day for her entailed getting dressed in the morning and undressed at night. To stave off the shivers, she wore under her day clothes a garment of one kind or another that she didn't have to take off at night. In other words, always clad in some article of clothing, like ski underwear, she avoided stripping naked in the cold. Reminds me of cowboys' (and my grandfather's, for that matter) legendary long johns.

Keeping the feet warm is my biggest winter challenge. To combat frigid tootsies, I wear socks 24/7. Before getting into bed at night, I don special footwear: ratty, dingy, old athletic socks. (In case of my demise while sleeping, I've requested my husband Mikey to remove these heirlooms before the officials come for my body. This timely gesture will save embarrassment to the family.) I know wearing socks to bed is a total sexual turn-off, but what's more important—preventing frozen feet or arousing my husband after 43 years of marriage? At my age, passion's flames do not warm my feet on a blustery, freezing night.

Another way I fend off cold is by taking a scalding shower. My body retains heat for at least 20 minutes after I emerge from the shower. I even sweat profusely. Rivulets of perspiration run from under my breasts to my waist, which anymore is not that great a distance. I've never before in my life faced this problem. All these years previously I've been totally unsympathetic to my husband's grousing about continuous sweating after a shower. He turns the bedroom ceiling fan to full speed and stands clad in his skimpy jockey shorts under it in an attempt to cool down. He's always claimed that he couldn't fit physical exercise into his pre-work morning routine; it took too much time given the necessary showering and the subsequent sweating ordeal. No more do I nag Mikey about morning work-outs.

I guess I shouldn't complain about the occasional hot flashes and the post-shower body heat. In a sense they counterbalance the extreme cold I feel at times. Once in a while I suffer chills that don't abate without resorting to excessive layering, wearing a thermal coat indoors or getting into my car and cranking the heat way up. The car acts as my own little personal sauna under this circumstance. Of course, my husband can't be with me in the car when I take advantage of this instant heat. In the first place, he seems to be naturally hot at all times. In the second place, Mikey would demand that I turn the car heater down immediately. I've learned after all these years to accommodate my husband's wishes, at least in some areas.

Perhaps a compromise for Mikey and me would be the purchase of one of those newer-model, behemoth vehicles, like a Ford Explorer, that boasts seats individually adjustable for both heat and cold. What a godsend for couples, as well as for women my age: a hot seat to warm us in winter and a cool seat to assuage hot flashes.

Chapter Two

"No, I'm not retarded; I just can't hear and I don't remember."

...in after years,
When these wild ecstasies shall be matured
Into a sober pleasure; when thy mind
Shall be a mansion for all lovely forms,
Thy memory be as a dwelling-place
For all sweet sounds and harmonies; oh! then,
If solitude, or fear, or pain, or grief,
Should be thy portion, with what healing thoughts
Of tender joy wilt thou remember me, ...
—from William Wordsworth's "Lines" (aka "Tintern Abbey"), 1798

My "wild ecstasies" are matured all right, but memory? My memory is *too* mature. Sometimes my brain does surprise and delight me, though, when some detail or event from deep within its recesses comes to the fore. But all too often the synapse just doesn't fire; it smolders. We're all familiar with the now proverbial "senior moment," the "can't remember @#$%" syndrome/CRS. For the life of us, we can't recall some word, date, fact, joke, our best friend's name, whatever, when it's relevant. Instead, we remember later and joltingly blurt it out to our husbands, grown children, friends, yoga instructor, whomever, regardless of time or place. This "golden years eureka" occurs in the middle of the night, in the middle of a conversation, in the shower, hours later, two days later, or weeks later. We're just so thrilled at having remembered we can't hold back. Besides, if we don't immediately spit it out, we may forget again.

What else do we forget? How about where we put our dentures? My husband, who's in the dental lab business, told me two of the biggest reasons for denture/partial repairs, both of which are related to memory problems. The first occurs when a person takes out her partials, places them in a tissue, forgets she put them there, and throws the value-laden tissue into the hearth fire. The acrylic partial melts, but fortunately the metal alloy doesn't unless a temperature reaches 2600 degrees F, heat far more intense than that generated in a home fireplace. Thus the patient can bring in the charred remains for repair. The other reason is not putting partials out of reach of the dog or cat who promptly gnaws on them. Yum, tastes like chicken. Pets cannot chew through a chrome/cobalt framework, so again, the patient can bring what's left into the dentist to have a repair done.

Speaking of pets, one of my best friends wasn't paying attention to what she was doing and swallowed her dog's heartworm medicine instead of her own Zocor. After her initial panic and an emergency call to her physician, she survived quite nicely. Such treasured friends help me retain my sanity in that, with humor if not swallowed pride, they share memory lapse anecdotes. My friends and I have talked about the book and television stories that we've read or watched, then re-read and re-watched because, try as we might, we can't remember the endings. An English literature Ph.D. friend says nowadays it's not unusual for her to be well into a book before she discovers that she's already read it. It happens to the best and brightest of us.

You know the stale joke about the reason old ladies should not have babies? Because they can't remember where they put them. C'est moi. I unintentionally leave closet doors open, lights on, underpants in the middle of the bathroom floor. When preparing our family Easter dinner this year, I went to the basement to put food in our spare refrigerator only to discover about a dozen shriveled, brownish, hard-as-rocks little balls, some with mildew. Those barely recognizable hard objects were, once upon a time, fresh, delectable navel oranges. Last Christmas I had stored those beautiful oranges in the fruit drawer of the downstairs fridge because there wasn't room for them in the one in our kitchen. What can I say? I forgot.

    Speaking of Christmas, I've reached the point where I'm going to have to label every gift I store in my Santa closet. I've always considered myself quite clever because I begin buying Xmas presents for next year immediately after the most recent Christmas. As the weeks and months progress, the new purchases multiply in my Xmas storage cupboard. The system worked well in the past, but now I get confused over what I've bought for whom, which gifts are brand new, which ones I bought too many of in the past and haven't figured out what to do with the remainder yet, and which ones to "re-gift." You know about re-gifting, I'm sure—it comes under the guise of recycling, like tissue paper, fancy ribbon, and gift bags. My daughter taught me this ingenious, money-saving trick. It appeals to a lot of folks in my generation who were raised to "waste not, want not." This is how it works: you take the presents other kind folks have given you that you don't want or can't use—for example, two decks of elegant bridge cards with minuscule numbers and symbols I can no longer make out—and pawn them off on somebody else. Everybody's happy; we're saving the environment, and most of the re-gifts are, after all, nice to receive. Some of the gifts however—like the small plastic elephant sculpture—I just need to bundle up and take to Goodwill. Regardless of whether the gift is recycled or one newly purchased by me, I must start labeling everything, or I'm likely to be embarrassed. It's possible that I've re-gifted an article to the original giver, and she's too kind to let on. My only hope in such a case is that she doesn't remember either.

Antiquated men naturally have the same kinds of memory problems as we women. My husband recently left the water spigot in the bathroom running full stream for a minimum of 1½ hours before I discovered his lapse. Thinking in terms of his future verbal retaliation if I should pull a similar stunt, I didn't rub it in.

For jogging my memory, photos and scrapbooks have become a godsend to me. I'm incredibly fortunate in having traveled to every continent save Antarctica (I loathe an icy environment), either in a professional capacity or on vacation. I'm not so fortunate, however, in being able to recall all the wonderful details of my journeys. For instance, somebody recently asked me about one of our trips, "What cruise line did you use?" Well, I was clueless. I raced home, pulled out the appropriate scrapbook and, *voila*, there was the name "Carnival."

Years ago some of my female colleagues/dear friends and I started a "Birthday Divas" practice of throwing a potluck dinner party on the occasion of each of our birthdays. Being inculcated with the dress code of my coevals, I certainly don't want to commit the *faux pas* of wearing the same outfit two celebrations in a row. But there's no way I can retain from month to month what I wear at each b'day dinner. Providently, we divas keep a scrapbook of photos, as well as some choice, hilarious, merciless cards about aging, from each get-together. As the guardian and compiler of the scrapbook, I have handy access to it. If I couldn't consult our photo album, my fashion statement would translate into rather pathetic redundancy.

By the way, have you heard "Happy Birthday" sung with non-traditional lyrics to the tune of the "Volga Boatmen?" One of my favorite female friends found this version on the internet, if I recall correctly (we can't be too sure of my recall, though, now can we?!). As a dirge, it's especially cruel to us oldies but goodies. But it's meant as a joke, and we use this version to tease each other. It goes something like this:

> Happy birthday, oh happy birthday,
> Pain and sickness in the air,
> Death and dying everywhere,
> But happy birthday, oh happy birthday.

I'm surprised I even remember that little ditty given all the items which long ago slipped my mind. For instance, do you remember where you've filed all your important documents? I'm perfectly aware that I own U.S. Savings Bonds, but it dawned on me the other day: "Just how many U.S. Savings Bonds do I have and where are they?" To find out, I had to plow through boxes at home and make a trip to the bank. In retirement it's imperative that we keep up with such things, right?

So that I don't have to constantly remember where I put my eyeglasses, I keep a pair in every room in the house. Before you draw the conclusion that I've spent a fortune on prescription glasses, let me assure you that all of mine are five- to fifteen-dollar, discount store magnifying ones. I'm extremely grateful that, SO FAR, I can read without Rx eyeglasses—well, as long as there's sufficient light. Forget those romantic candlelit dinners in our favorite restaurant—who can decipher the menu? Also, Mikey fusses when I plan a dinner party by candlelight. He prefers to see what he's eating. Notwithstanding our "night blindness," my ophthalmologist says the magnifying glasses are fine for me now but advises me to keep coming in for check-ups. I hope I can remember to make a yearly appointment.

My cherished baby sister, a foreign language teacher for nigh on 40 years, attests that she now forgets names and facts in three different tongues. But we seniors shouldn't berate ourselves too harshly regarding memory loss; forgetting is by no means an exclusive trait of the elderly. Multitudes of young people misplace their keys, jackets, credit cards, iPhones, and Blackberries, to name a few items. We can be smug with this thought: if youngsters are frustrated now—wait until they've lived long enough for data inundation of an exhausted brain.

When one is aged, though, one finally and truly can empathize with those who've been labeled "handicapped" throughout their lives. The public often perceives those of us who deviate physically from the cultural ideal, i.e., young and perfectly healthy, as mentally deficient. The following is an illustration. Even with technologically sophisticated hearing aides, I often still can't clearly understand what a person is saying, especially if there's a lot of background noise, or if the person is a soft-spoken soprano, or is speaking with her back to me. In an effort to comprehend, I may pause for a few seconds to try to figure out the words from context, or I'll ask the person to repeat what she's said. Many times the speaker will respond impatiently to me in either a patronizing or otherwise condescending manner. Not too long ago, an uninformed, insensitive, young salesperson grimaced rudely when I asked her to repeat an instruction for programming phone numbers in my new cell phone. I retorted in a rather ugly fashion (behavior normally not in character for me): "Trust me. I'm not stupid, just hard of hearing."

Last week at the grocery store I apologized to the older checkout clerk for not hearing clearly what she had said. She smiled at me with her gracious, kind reply, "Welcome to our age."

My husband's auditory problems are much more severe than mine. He can't hear the toilet running, let alone me. We both have difficulty discerning exact words over the phone; even with my hearing aids, I haven't mastered phone conversation. Mikey and I are trying to overcome that aggravation by (a) replacing our outdated land phones with those equipped for high volume and (b) setting our cell phones on high volume or speaker-phone. We're getting there, but it takes time, money, and thought.

Mikey, known for his sadistic teasing at times, used to pull a nasty trick on his sweet, darling mother who wore hearing aids.

Having lived through the Great Depression, his frugal mom saved on batteries by turning off her hearing aids when she was home alone. She kept them in her ears, though, so that if someone came, she could quickly turn them on. At lunchtime from work my mischievous husband would walk into her house, where she had so lovingly prepared him food, and start mouthing words to her. She'd immediately cup the side of her ear with the palm of her hand, repeatedly, to try to get a sound. Of course, she was trying to ascertain if her batteries were dead or just turned off. Her dastardly son found her futilely banging the side of her head side-splittingly funny. Luckily for Mikey she loved him unconditionally, had a good sense of humor, and was forgiving of her son's antics.

Sometimes when my husband, the stereotypic macho male who refuses to succumb to hearing aids, and I, or some of our other hearing-impaired friends, are trying to have a conversation, we personify those jokes where everybody misunderstands everybody else. It's reminiscent of the bygone gossip game where the first person whispers a sentence into the next person's ear, and by the time the sentence is recited aloud by the last person in line, it's hardly recognizable as the original thought. When we mishear and thus misunderstand each other, I'm also reminded somehow of the old Bud Abbot and Lou Costello "Who's on first?" routine.

It's great comedy. We gotta' laugh.

Chapter Three

Preening

> I believe that society doesn't encourage men to be more concerned with their hairstyles because preoccupation with superficial physical attraction is seen as a sign of personal insecurity, character weakness and a lack of deeper worth. And I think this makes sense. Women pay a big price for trying to look as desirable as they possibly can.
> —Marilyn vos Savant, in "Ask Marilyn," *Parade Magazine*, April 2, 2000

You may not agree with Marilyn, who, according to the Guinness Book of World Records, possesses an I.Q. of 228! I think she's right, especially regarding how much time it takes to "look desirable." With every passing day of my life, time becomes more of a precious commodity, and I don't want to fritter it away on trivial pursuits.

For better or worse, social scientists have substantiated that both men and women are judged initially on appearances. Taller men and prettier women are at an advantage in social settings, whether it's in politics, business, or the dating game. Our culture puts far greater pressure on females than males to look attractive. Even though men are starting to get more of their share, the frequency of television cosmetics commercials targeting females—such as those for Olay skin "rejuvenation," L'Oreal "because we're worth it" hair coloring, and Cover Girl make-up—attest to the predominance of that gender market.

The vast majority of my female coevals were taught that beauty is a woman's most valuable asset. Coming of age, we constantly were judged on our looks. Women in my age group were socialized to believe that our best chances for a good life lay in attracting and marrying a man with a good income; consequently, we were eager to please the male species. Many of us senior females remain stuck in this mode.

For men, pleasing women may entail a different challenge. A silly corollary occurs to me from the handsomely framed instructions an acquaintance of mine hangs on the wall over her toilet tank. It reads, "I aim to please. You aim too, please." I might add that one of the salient difficulties for an old man is his aim. You may interpret this last sentence any way you please.

For women, society emphasizes pulchritude. My sister has been blessed with stunning looks since the day she was born. Although true beauty is a joy forever, I wonder if it's a bit difficult for her now that she's over 60 that not every head turns when she enters the room. I've never been beautiful, so I don't know anything about that kind of disappointment. Discouraging to me, however, is how rapidly in the years since I turned 65 that my appearance has gone downhill. Sometimes the change for the worse is so fast it's like an evil genie has been let out of the bottle, looked at me, pronounced "Kazam," and just like that I go from not looking my age one day to looking geriatric the next.

Some women abhor telling or admitting to their age. Some female friends try to give the impression that they are much younger than you although they are not. Do you have a friend who is, say, only 1 ½ years younger than you but always insinuates that she is way younger?

Throngs of women, and more and more men these days, spend billions (yes, billions) to inject poison into their skin or to have some kind of cosmetic surgery to regain the facade of their lost youth. Sociologist Laurie Essig (*American Plastic*, 2010) found in interviews with plastic surgery candidates that they were going under the knife in an attempt to secure both mates and jobs. We're familiar with the "find or keep a partner" motivation for cosmetic surgery, but, barring the "tinsel town" industry, job market advantage lends a new twist to the reasons for "beauty at any cost." Most of us are familiar too with plastic surgery cases gone wrong—a permanently weeping eye or a sagging cheek. Imagine going to all that trouble and expense only to have eyeballs protruding grotesquely out of their sockets or a smile so tight it threatens to break the face. Two cases in point: veteran actor Kirk Douglas (Mike Douglas' dad) and his younger counterpart Burt Reynolds. I adore both these actors, always have, but I'm sorry, their respective face lifts make them look like space aliens.

Why do some of us aging folks try to look glamorous on the exterior when our interiors are becoming irreparably unimpressive? In my opinion, trying desperately to appear young when we're not is false advertising. We can't deliver what we seem to promise.

Not that I don't sympathize. For one my age, looking in the mirror can be dreadful. (I suppose one solace of failing eyesight is a more camouflaged, and hence kinder, view of wrinkles.) I too am looking for miracles as is evidenced by my increasing collection of "age-defying" lotions. I resort to four different kinds of facial creams, not to mention my practice of slathering moisturizer all over my body either before or after I shower.

It's difficult concealing one's face from the public, but I do try to cover body parts as much as possible. In this regard, do burka-clad or veiled Muslim women enjoy an advantage? (I need to look more closely into Islamic culture.) The only time I disrobe in front of another human being is when I treat myself to a massage, but

I'm increasingly embarrassed to go. I asked my masseuse one time if most of her clients are relatively young. She answered in the affirmative. I know why. I ask myself how much longer I should request a massage gift card for Christmas from my husband.

First, I'm totally disenchanted with my spider veins. For the last few years, although shorter skirts are in style, my skirts have become gradually longer and longer as the broken veins creep farther and farther down my legs. I've tried to explain to my current ballroom dance teacher why in our dance recitals I cannot wear costumes that expose my legs. And, no, I can't begin to find any hose opaque enough to cover all those blue streaks. There should be new rules for dance competitions allowing older women to wear slacks, no matter the style of dance. I suppose it never occurred to Arthur Murray that some senior ladies might like to continue to dance Latin routines if only they weren't required to don skimpy attire. Bare midriffs, short skirts, sleeveless tops and décolletage won't win any prizes in dance showcases or any other venue for most of us "women of a certain age" (whatever the hell that age is).

Might I point out, for instance, the loose skin, most commonly under the neck, called a dewlap, as well as that under the upper arms. That is to say, some of us become fowl-like: our neck resembles a turkey gobbler's, and we've sprouted chicken wings. Nora Ephron bemoans this kind of phenomena in her book, *I Feel Bad About My Neck* (2008). In sleeveless blouses we look like we're getting ready to take off. My sister describes what happens to our skin in old age this way: the skin starts to pull away from the bone like well-cooked meat and just hangs.

The tiny, mole-like growths called "tags" that seem to multiply overnight aren't lovely either. I used to go occasionally to my dermatologist to have a mole removed, not for the serious threat of a melanoma for all that sun worshipping I engaged in when it was the "in" thing to do, but because of the unattractiveness. Now I can't afford to trot to his office often enough to get rid of the things.

My diminished body hair also poses an aesthetic threat. Instead of concern about putting on clean underwear before I venture out (you know—in case of an accident and being shamed in the emergency room), the possible public discovery of my unshaved legs gives me pause. I forget to shave. Not that I have much to shave. I recall an acquaintance telling his mother her hairless (old) body reminded him of a skinned wiener. *C'est moi.* I'm shedding patches of hair on my head, rarely need to shave my armpits, and sport only sparsely scattered, longish hairs over my shins. What's to shave? That's why I forget. Nonetheless, for a well-groomed look, those sparse long hairs need to be cropped.

I suppose it could be worse. For some of us oldsters, hair grows in all the wrong places, as in my husband's nostrils. Because she's super observant, my daughter sounds off about his overgrown nasal hair in need of a trim. A male colleague of mine declares that we are all born with a certain number of hairs. He contends that as we age, we become increasingly hairless but with vestiges in odd places. This tendency gives expanded meaning to the expression "a wild hair."

Bill Cosby in 1988 gave us *Time Flies,* his humorous view on aging. As you might expect from this wonderful comedian, actor, and humanitarian, it's a delightful little book. One part I remember quite well from his musings is the sketch about gray hairs—on his head, in his eyebrows, and most hilariously, in his pubic area. He describes how initially he carefully plucked the occasional white hair in his private parts but gave up the practice as the removal of each new tell-tale bristle became too time consuming.

Do you ever tire of grooming? I'm even weary of daily bathing. I like to postpone it a day (or two). Bathing has become a bit of an ordeal, particularly the requisite slathering of my entire body with cream afterwards. Cream assuages the sere look as well as my itching to death. I should follow Doris Day's (you know her as the perennial virgin in old Hollywood romantic comedies) example and grease down every night with petroleum jelly. But who can afford petroleum derivative products these days? Furthermore, how does one wash Vaseline out of bed linens and pajamas? Unlike most of humanity, Doris could probably afford to throw away her slimy night threads.

Somehow neither showers nor baths fit easily into my schedule. In the mornings I don't want to squander what little energy I still possess to bathe. I have more important matters to attend to, such as babysitting my precious grandchildren or practicing my piano. Come bedtime, I'm too exhausted to crawl into the tub.

I'm pretty sick of fixing my hair too. How many times have I coiffed it? Why couldn't I have been blessed with a gorgeous head of curly, thick hair. How many cans of hairspray have I used? I feel guilty about the destruction of the ozone layer, yet I persist in my hairspray dependence. My hair has absolutely no body. It's straight as the proverbial stick. I can't wear my hair naturally straight (or long) because that style is unbecoming to my chipmunk cheeks and long, aging face. Decades ago the famous model Cheryl Tiegs declared that if she were allowed only one beauty product on a deserted isle, her choice would be cheek blusher. Mine would be hair spray. Give me a can of hair spray, and I can create a hairstyle becoming to me, come hail or high water.

Many of us born in the 40s and 50s to families of modest means have acquired a repertoire of do-it-yourself cosmetic skills. We've lived long enough to have mastered hair curlers of all sizes and shapes, curling irons, hot rollers, and blow dryers. In the 60s and 70s some of us actually used an iron and ironing board to perfectly straighten our long tresses. A number of us can give ourselves a passable haircut and decent style, even color or a perm. However, it's probably better for us gray or white hairs, skill or no skill, to visit a salon for any potent chemical applications. An error at our age can be costly, even hilariously grotesque. We could resemble Ms. Frankenstein, or we could be aptly referred to as Ms. Blue

Hair. In a worst-case scenario, our heretofore thinning hair could completely fall out.

I kept hoping that when my hair turned gray it would have more body, frizz even. Still my hair just lies there, it just dies there, as in Nat King Cole's (Natalie's father) love song, "Mona Lisa." I've heard scores of people lament, "Oh, my hair is so frizzy now that it's turned gray that I can't do a thing with it." I should be so lucky. In any case, I take heart in the fact that we older women somehow manage. An hour's worth of preening in the bathroom can produce an amazing transformation.

Besides grooming, there's the issue of shopping for decently fashionable but appropriate-for-the-older-woman clothes. Good luck. You'd think with the millions of us still alive and the even greater millions of baby boomers following right behind, clothing designers and manufacturers would wise up to the potentially huge market waiting out there. My body looks pathetic, if not ludicrous, in the latest (youthful) styles—spandex shirts, short shorts, plunging necklines and skin-tight jeans. But I don't want to dress in frumpy polyester either. Is it too much to ask for apparel designed between these two extremes? At least we have stretch denim now.

And thank goodness for dressy flip-flops (another oxymoron). Even supple-boned young women injure themselves in today's 4-inch stilettos. One of my beloved venerable friends, now deceased, inspired me for a variety of reasons, including her practical dress style. She happened to be one of the pillars of our community and wealthy enough to purchase the most elegant of clothes. Nonetheless, what was her regular footwear, including what she wore with formal garb? She always wore sneakers, mostly black Rockports. She made an exception for dress-up occasions, but only in colors: she had one pair of her sneakers spray painted silver and another pair spray painted gold, providing "glamorous" shoes befitting her more elegant ensembles.

I've always had size problems with dresses and blouses because my boobs are a little large in proportion to the rest of my frame. My 36 DD chest size has been both a blessing and a curse for me. On the one hand, I've never needed or wanted breast implants; on the other, finding tops that don't make me look like a streetwalker continues to be a challenge.

It's not just me. Concern over boobs, regardless of size, shape, or age, pervades our American culture. At our divas' birthday parties (which I refer to in Ch. 2) we exchange, with peals of self-conscious laughter, more than our share of "boob cards," i.e., those depicting the chest problems of us aging women. Here are some of the lines: "With every year that passes, our cups runneth over." "Go braless…it pulls the wrinkles out of your face." And there are the revised lyrics that go,

> Do your boobs hang low,
> Do they wobble to and fro,
> Can you tie 'em in a knot,
> Can you tie 'em in a bow,
> Can you throw 'em over your shoulder
> Like a military soldier,
> Do your boobs—hang—low?
> —(anonymous)

These days, in addition to the "forward boob look" (or "downward look" as some view it) I have to contend with rolls of fat on my back. In selecting tops, I opt for a loose garment, usually not in the latest fashion, which makes me look even fatter in my old age.

Let me forewarn you that what I'm about to describe next may "gross you out," as those of us in the autumn of life used to say when we were young. Here goes. I still choose to wear colorful cotton Jockey underpants. I pick various colors because white panties bore me. Cotton fabric breathes and is more hygienic than synthetic materials. However, I always buy the sleek French cut panties—perhaps not the most tasteful style for hiding my cellulite—because full bloomers accentuate my upper thigh saddle bags.

Even more obscene, though, at least to his male friends, is the fact that my husband continues to wear Jockey's briefs for men. Mikey tips the scale a little on the heavy side for one thing. For another, his body shows wear and tear, just as mine does. On a golf trip a few years back, his buddies teased him unmercifully as he was undressing for bed in the motel room they were sharing. One of them asked, "How much do you think Jockey would pay you NOT to wear their briefs?" I dare not undress in front of my female friends.

By contrast to my litany of physical flaws, I happen to have at least half a dozen women friends between 60 and 85 who still possess quite good looks. When we vacation at the beach together, these women without a moment's hesitation put on their bathing suits and head for the ocean. Those lucky devils retain nice figures and lovely legs. I, on the other hand, show up on the beach fully dressed even if the thermometer is hovering around 95 degrees Fahrenheit or above. I wear cotton capris (formerly known by us older folks as pedal pushers or beachcomber pants), a shirt with sleeves, and my Panama hat (I use Retin-A to prevent wrinkles and can't expose my face to the sun for any length of time). Some of us still have it. Some of us don't.

Many of us older ladies attempt to "still have it" by sporting drop-dead gorgeous fingernails and toenails. In droves we beat a path to one of our local nail salons (most of which in our little burg are Asian operated) for acrylic nail extensions polished with dazzling colors. Afterwards we flash our foxy nails with the youngest and the finest.

For those of you who feel more haggard than foxy, not to worry; we're still marvelous, Darling. One of my closest friends recently threw a "crone party" in celebration of her favorite women. Research she had come across earlier revealed that the term "crone" historically designated a very wise, older woman who commanded great respect in her community. If someone should disparagingly refer to you as an "old crone," just flash them a knowing smile. You can dismiss the wicked witch, harridan stereotype. Yes, the reference is unkind. More importantly, it's mistaken.

Chapter Four

OMG! TARSU IMHO[1]

Children are now tyrants….they no longer rise when elders enter the room. They contradict their parents, chatter before company, gobble up dainties at the table, cross their legs, and tyrannize over their teachers.
—Socrates, 5th century B.C.E.

Sound familiar? That's because every older generation, going back to Greek civilization or further, has groused that young people are going to the dogs. You know a superannuated person such as I must have at least one forum, one chapter in this case, in which she can complain about how bad things are now in comparison to how wonderful things used to be. (You can skip this bitchin'[2] chapter if you want, you know, although I promise not to spin any yarns about tramping through snow for miles to school.)

So here go my pet peeves. Many people today can neither write well nor spell correctly. Due to the pervasive influence of television and movies, the communication succinctness demanded by texting and email, and a lack of reading which can help develop vocabulary, many in the younger generations resort to profanity instead of articulation. Furthermore, minors are encouraged through the media, not to mention their contemporaries, to act and dress in ways quite inappropriate for their maturity level. Last, but by no means least on my list, hordes of children are raised with little discipline at home or in school. I'll expound upon these issues one by one.

My first gripe concerns grammar. Before I begin my tirade about incorrect language use, however, I must make a disclaimer. In this book you'll come across a lot of contractions, some incomplete sentences, slang, and other broken rules for "proper" grammar. I use these forms not out of ignorance but for effect. My only defense is that I want for this particular subject matter to write in a casual style, one that more closely resembles the way we normally converse. Perhaps you think that I, granting myself such compositional privilege, have no right to criticize others. In response let me quote one of my favorite authors, Dorothy L. Sayers, "Time and trouble will tame an advanced young woman. But an advanced older woman is uncontrollable by any force." I'm inclined to do as I please even if it means self-contradiction.

Having laid out my defense, I shall proceed to reproach others' misuse of the King's English.

Who knew we'd live to see the day when the objective case in English would cease to exist, at least in its proper grammatical place. As my sagacious friend, a former college literature professor, reminds me, language is a living, moving phenom (slang purposely used here for illustrative purposes, and granted, slang too has been around since the beginning of history). In other words, language patterns change over time. O.K., I buy that, but it still grates when I hear, "Are you going to the movies with she and I?" Or how about, "Me and him bought concert tickets"?

I have my suspicions about the origins of such improper grammar. I distinctly remember my brother, eighteen years younger than I, telling me he chose to take "Literature in Cinema" for his required English course (!!) in high school back in the late seventies. In my day, every high school English course reinforced conventional grammar rules. Plus, we had to diagram sentences until we could do it in our sleep. After all the social protests of the sixties decade, English instruction started emphasizing creativity rather than rote grammar. School systems ceased requiring established grammar usages across the curriculum; droves of students stopped learning "correct" grammar. We purists are now definitely in the minority and are apparently dying out at an alarming rate.

Masses of young people these days can't write a decent paragraph. They don't begin to understand what a topic sentence is. Again, creativity in writing is rewarded, and despite my carping, I do acknowledge its importance. One good departure from the 20th century: one rarely encounters any more "stream of consciousness" writing assignments in English classes. (Recently a zealous member in our book group elected to have us read James Joyce's *Ullysses*. Some of our members flatly refused to do it but showed up regardless the next month, sipped their Chardonnay, and listened politely to the discussion by those masochists who had dutifully read the book.)

And spelling! Some people never learn to spell correctly. Further confusion results from the pervasiveness of digital devices capable of tweeting, e-mailing, texting, and even spell-check. Look at billboards, marquees, menus, ads, etc.—does the widely public misspelling, as well as the grammatical errors, make you cringe? There's the *Alright Parking* lot sign downtown, as well as the sign that instructs us to *Drive Thru* at the dry cleaners. Have you ever eaten "beefstake" or bought "iceburg" lettuce? The first item was listed on a menu, the second in a grocery ad in my hometown. My husband and I were recently assured in writing by a household moving company that our china plates would be tightly "wraped." Near Smith Mountain Lake in Virginia I spotted a roadside ad for *The Martin's Florist*. I doubt if there is only one Martin who possesses that flower shop. Similarly, I saw *The Boyd's* written in large, cursive letters in the sand at North Myrtle Beach, South Carolina. Is this a family of one?

Curse words are used liberally, especially in many movie scripts and stand-up comedy routines on television. Do people have such limited vocabularies that they must resort to profanity, or are they simply trying to relate to a dummied-down audience? Part of the problem has to be that multitudes hold nothing sacred anymore, so we hear more and more erstwhile taboo words. Following our generation's various cultural revolutions of the sixties and seventies, some folks turned to formerly forbidden words out of defiance of authority. Think George Carlin and his "7 words you can't say on TV" routine—bless his brilliance. Today those words pepper the skits on the Comedy channel as well as the dialogues of HBO, Encore and Showtime channel movies, for examples.

You can believe my father-in-law was truly of the older generation when I tell you that back in 1982 he walked out of the theater in disgust at the foul language in *On Golden Pond*. Mikey and I had recommended the movie to him. We thought he'd enjoy not only the story about an elderly retired professor and his wife but also the marvelous acting of "the two olds" (the current nickname for grandparents in China), Katharine Hepburn and Henry Fonda. In terms of cursing, that movie can't hold a candle to most movies today. I wonder if my father-in-law would even walk into a theater whose marquee featured *Meet the Fockers*? Of course, "fockers" is not even a thinly disguised take-off on the "big F" word, so favored by the rebellious, gifted comedian Richard Pryor for one, not to mention Lenny Bruce, the father of all obscenities.

Television programming includes such shows as *The Simpsons*, one of those cartoon vehicles which allows dialogues that censors won't grant real actors (or will they?). Meanwhile parents pay no attention to children tuning in to these "harmless" little cartoons—harmless if you exclude respectful attitudes, strict morals, and civility. Then there's Miley Cyrus, aka Hannah Montana, once widely popular children's TV star and role model, revealed on national entertainment news taking a real-live "hit" from a bong.

Another educator friend of mine, an astute observer of human behavior, contends that there is no civility anymore, that people no longer adhere to manners or show simple consideration of others. I readily confess she's my contemporary. Together we grump about the passing of the good 'ol days.

In many families, both parents work outside the home, and in a significant number of those cases, supervision and teaching of children have diminished to the point that children don't learn how to behave in a civil manner at home or in public. For a great many families, two full-time incomes are absolutely necessary economically. Those families deserve empathy; they have no options. Perhaps for a minority of dual- income couples, both parents work outside the home less for financial reasons than out of personal preference. One can understand professional commitment. On the other hand, in U.S. society where materialism abounds, adults may voluntarily work to purchase such items as a new outdoor deck. Some may work outside the home to escape the arduous task of staying home full-time raising the children. Some of us are not cut out for taking care of young children; that's understandable. Then who's parenting? This is not to say that parents who are gone from home 40+ hours a week can't be good parents; quite the contrary. There are also excellent, professional childcare providers available. It's just that a pet complaint of mine is a lack of recognition in our society that child rearing deserves utmost priority. Seriously.

The lack of proper attention to children contributes to the decreasing civility in our culture. I'll share one, perhaps trite, example. As a former professor in a small, expensive liberal arts college, I sometimes (and somewhat hesitantly) joined my students for a meal. Usually every time the darlings and I broke bread together there was one student, college age, mind you, who chomped with her mouth open or didn't know how to use a napkin. Show me a child of this age who is not familiar with a modicum of table graces, and I can show you parents, wealthy or not, who never took the time to teach, or pay attention to, their child's table manners. Call me prissy.

Recently on the popular television show *Family Feud*, contestants were asked to name places where parents assume a laissez-faire attitude towards their children's behavior. Some of the answers offended my prickly nature. For instance, near the top of the list of places where offspring are allowed to run amuck was "restaurant." Are there times when you're eating out that you want to throttle both the parents and their little hellions when the latter are roaming at will, tripping servers, hiding under tables, or yelling? The lack of consideration of the dining pleasure of others ruffles my worn-out tail feathers.

The well-known anthropologist Margaret Mead envisioned rightly that married couples before being permitted to bear and raise children should qualify for a parenting license.

Naturally as a snappish elder, I also beef about how young people dress nowadays. (You'll understand the play on the word "beef" in the context I'm about to describe.) Did you see Lady Gaga in 2010 in her appearance at the MTV Music Awards Show? You may not watch MTV, but countless young people do; they watch, and they absorb. The "Lady" was attired from head to foot in raw, red meat. A strip of raw meat adorned her head, while a meat "dress," a meat "purse," and meat "shoes" rounded out her ensemble. I concede this is an extreme example.

When my two sisters and I were growing up, my fuddydud (yes, very dated slang) father tried to patrol, as best he could, how we dressed. Once he made me come back into the house and change slacks because he thought mine were too tight. They weren't. He also threw a fit when he saw my older sister and me as teenagers sunbathing, lying on our stomachs with our bathing suit tops pulled down—we wanted brown backs from our shoulders to our waists, no strap lines—perfectly logical. Besides, our private backyard precluded public exhibition. I think Dad harbored some serious sexual repression.

By my father's standards, young women dress practically naked these days, right? Is current youth fashion, which reveals generous cleavage as well as butt cracks, provocative? Or do parents believe that children are so innocent that sexuality is not an issue? Ha. (I remember vividly my first "wet dream." I must've been around 9 or 10. The two players in my dream happened to be frogs—of all things, I kid you not—but believe me, they were going at it.) Or are we so gender-liberated now that both males and females eschew responsibility for the opposite sex's reaction to their super sensual attire?

The media feeds on blatant sexuality. Have you seen that delicious Beyonce?

Controversy exists over whether young women should face criminal charges for sending their own naked images over the internet or phone. Is nothing private now? Probably not. Thanks to huge data banks, your lunch, purchases, occupation, marital status, salary, place of residence, religious preference—you name it—it's all a matter of public record. Contributing to online revelations are sites such as Facebook, MySpace, and Twitter, where participants tend to tell all. Lawbreakers watch for personal info posted routinely, enabling them to steal identity or to safely enter a home and commit robbery. In a very real sense, we invite Orwell's "Big Brother" to watch us.

Woe and begone, bitchin' chapter.

NOTES

1. These are texting acronyms. OMG! = Oh, my God!; TARSU = Things are really screwed up; and IMHO = In my humble opinion. If you're not familiar with texting, the popular mode of communication, especially among the younger generation, check out www.textingdictionaryofacronyms.com.

2. I'm using "bitchin" in this context to mean complaining; in modern "street speak" "bitchin" means "cool," or "awesome."

Chapter Five

Sex

> What most persons consider a virtue, after the age of 40 is simply a loss of energy.
> —Voltaire (1694-1778)

H-m-m, in my old age am I virtuous because of my sexual abstention? Or have I simply run out of energy? For many of my cohorts, sex ranks right up there with death and taxes as an inescapable concern. Some remain quite sexually active while others engage in fantasy or simply reminisce.

I remember as a young adult hearing our Methodist minister say that even though he and his wife were old, he still felt a tingle when their toes touched in bed. (This wouldn't have been a Baptist minister, right? A Baptist minister back in the sixties wouldn't broach, let alone expound upon, such a subject from the pulpit.) I appreciate the tingle factor now, but at the time, I recall reacting to his story with an amused smirk.

Although you don't need to be told this, and despite the young person's distaste, many elderly people enjoy a passionate sex life. The desire to "do it" is perennial, I suppose, or maybe some take to heart the admonishment by physicians and others to "use it or lose it."

Even in our dotage, sex can remain troublesome in one way or another. Sexual desire, possessiveness, competition, jealousy, and STDs can hound us to the grave. One does not cease to be human when one is old. The relationships in retirement communities, assisted living, and nursing facilities sometimes mimic those in Peyton Place (for you youngsters, *Peyton Place* is the title of a 1950s book, later made into a t.v. series, both sizzling with illicit affairs).

Years ago I saw a television documentary on sexual behavior in nursing homes. I recollect from that program this withered, ancient woman who routinely snuck off into the furnace room for a tryst with her male paramour, another old fossil. Interviewed, the elderly woman said she wouldn't and couldn't live without sex. Both the nursing home staff and relatives of the two "culprits" were scandalized at such behavior and wanted it stopped. Hey, we seniors have rights too.

Another t.v. program I watched about 10 years ago documented the occurrence of AIDS among sexually active older people in the United States. According to this show, elderly women were particularly at risk. Well beyond the age of conceiving and never suspecting their over-the-hill lovers as carriers of HIV, these women consented to unprotected sex. In most cases, they were shocked to discover 10 years later that they were infected.

My father, who survived to age 91 (Mama died 26 years before he did), fortunately never contracted an STD. Neither did he ever lose interest in sex. He remained feisty, literally until his dying day, in an independent living facility. The lovely complex where he lived for over a decade is, as statistically expected, populated by a far greater number of older women than men. Dad swore that some of the ladies regularly hit on him, but he wasn't interested: he declared them too old (!!). Of course, they were all around his age or younger. He rejected them because they were either physically unable to chauffeur him in his car (which he insisted upon keeping despite the fact that he was legally blind and not licensed to drive), they had a heart condition and were likely to die soon, or they couldn't dance. Yes, my father boogied, not too vigorously, but throughout his 80s.

He related some risqué tales about his involvement with a couple of his "younger" sweethearts who lived on the "outside." Handsome in his youth, as an old man he retained his vanity. He concluded that one of his girlfriends was lesbian because she wasn't willing to have intercourse with him. According to Dad, she would go only so far as to sit topless on his lap. Having known this practicing Christian woman fairly well, I didn't know whether to laugh or cry at such a revelation. At his retirement complex, he interpreted any act of kindness on the part of his various caretakers as flirtatious. I'm convinced that in his last years Dad dreamed or fantasized titillating affairs.

Whether residing in a facility for the aged or not, "casserole ladies," those women who hustle with their homemade food to the door of the most recent old widower, are legend. What are they really after? Sex? Perhaps in some cases. Companionship when dining out? Hey, I take a book to read when I'm eating by myself. An altruistic desire to serve as Florence Nightingale to an old man? Not bloody likely. Most probable: they're hoping to snag a bigger Social Security check, if not a lucrative portfolio. I'm not just being cynical here. The sole finances of an elderly woman often condemn her to a life of poverty. Why wouldn't she want to marry into greater means? The reality continues that men on average draw bigger salaries than women and hence receive larger Social Security and other types of retirement checks.

If it's a case of true love, elderly men and women nowadays often choose to forego the legal knot and move in together so they can each keep drawing their separate Social Security checks. People are not quite as prudish about relationships now as they once were. Thank goodness for the sexual revolution brought about by us retired hippies when we were in our prime.

Single mothers are, more often than not, especially strapped for cash. In such circumstances, older men may provide the financial security such younger women need. If an affluent old man wants to make a trade-off of "love" for money, that's his business (Hugh Hefner and his latest engagement to a mere child in her twenties come to mind). Same holds for older women. We know that wealthy matrons often hire young male escorts, if not marry them. Over a decade ago, when I took ballroom lessons at Arthur Murray, I vividly remember two incidences of the young man and the older woman. In one, a middle-aged dance student, also quite a prosperous business woman, married her twenty-something, meagerly salaried, studio instructor. Although both marriage and sexual liaisons between teachers and pupils are strictly *verboten* by the Arthur Murray franchise, persistently waltzing hip-to-hip can be physically arousing. So much so that it may lead to love (or lust, whichever). In a second May-December case from the studio, an attractive, solicitous, young man regularly accompanied an affluent, fragile, quite elderly woman at the Friday night dance parties. The dance staff concluded that he was a paid escort.

Within my comparatively younger crowd, the game-playing continues. We've all witnessed older women hitting on older men and vice-versa, sometimes whether the elders involved are single or married. A classic example: the supposedly loyal golf buddy, married, who hits on one of his foursome's wives. So much for friendship, eh? Who among us seniors hasn't heard of, or personally dealt with, these cheating-on-the-spouse episodes? One doesn't know whether to respond, "Oh, grow up," or to simply recognize that for some, "It ain't over 'til it's over." It's hard to pinpoint motive. Does one suffer from what I term a "late-life crisis?" Adulterous behavior could be a test to see if the aging person can still attract the opposite sex. Another reason for infidelity might be that what appears to be a long-lasting, solid marriage lacks some significant, fulfilling ingredient. Social biologists would argue that cheating men, regardless of age, are innately programmed to fling (another intended pun) their seed. Last, the cheating might involve a "cougar," the term for older, sexy, exceptionally attractive women. The assumption here is that such women are so irresistible and so hot-to-trot, weak men can't help themselves (!!). Of course I'm not sure how many of us senior women resemble Jane Fonda or Sophia Loren.

Cougars don't help the cases of women such as I who have always railed against the role of sex object. Besides, it takes too much time and effort when one is past one's prime to doll up for men.

Like so many pursuits these days, sex usually provokes only a flattened response in me. I'd rather be engaged in other, less physically demanding, endeavors—like playing bridge. Besides, I'm too persnickety. I don't like my privacy invaded or my bed linens messed up. (My dear husband deserves great sympathy.) My body is more sacred than ever. Don't laugh. Didn't your mother instill in you women that your body is a temple? I admit to a strong libido in my younger years. Now, however, I really prefer not to be desecrated.

My biggest problem is that with each passing year I have become increasingly independently minded; it's more and more difficult for me to compromise. If I'm going to have sex, I want it my way, to quote "old blue eyes" (that's Frank Sinatra to you folks who've been living in a cave for the last 70 years). If I can get up the nerve to go into one of those sex toy shops or to attend one of those sex toy home parties (I've heard about these from young women, but no one has ever invited me to one—could it be my age?!), or go on-line incognito, I can purchase a mechanical aid and take care of myself. I'm told there's quite a varied selection. Can't one just be left alone with one's vibrator? Why not? Everything else in our society is do-it-yourself.

Masturbation is a viable option. However, my generation grew up hearing from our parents that it results in horrible retribution. As regards females, the subject of sexual self-gratification rarely or never came up. It was believed that the average female didn't get sexually aroused enough to masturbate and/or that she was too obedient to break such a taboo. There was some validity to a female's adherence to rules back then, but later lab experiments sure blew the myth of the female's weak sexual response. Males, on the other hand (I just had to go with the pun), were warned repeatedly that they would grow hair in their palm or even go blind if they committed such an abominable sin. Even if any of these absurdities were true, in our golden years who cares? If something on my body looked abnormal, who would notice what with all the other physical peculiarities accompanying my decline.

Sometimes we oldies are simply no longer physically able to engage in sex. No wonder the guy in the sexual enhancement t.v. ads sports a perpetual grin. His problem is solved. Some of us older ladies grin more often too, now that modern medicine can relieve us of vaginal dryness.

With my increasing age I fear body function betrayal in an intimate situation. I totally relate to the following quote from John Banville's Man Booker prize-winning novel, *The Sea* (2005):

> ...I had held my physical self in no more than fond disgust, as most people do—hold their selves, I mean, not mine—tolerant, necessarily, of the products of my sadly inescapable humanity, the various effluvia, the eructations fore and aft, the gleet, the scurf, the sweat and other common leakages....(p. 51)

The passage, in keeping with this entire, wonderful novel on aging, remembrance, and the death of a spouse, is written in a completely serious tone. I, however, view this particular quotation with a perverted sense of humor for two reasons. First, I giggle sheepishly from thinking of "the products of my sadly inescapable humanity."

Second, I find Banville's rather obscure vocabulary, all in one sentence, a bit comical. Effluvia? It means odor. Eructations? Belches. Gleet? Nasal drip. Scurf? Dandruff or anything else scaly. "…[A]nd other common leakages" really cracks me up. What I realize to my chagrin is that these "products" occur with increasing frequency and in all the wrong settings as we age. I guess I want to preserve romance, but I don't feel I can during coitus. I can no longer depend on my deteriorating body to writhe in a becoming manner.

Chapter Six

Milk? When There's Wine?

Behold the rain which descends from the heaven upon our vineyards, there it enters the roots of the vines, to be changed into wine, a constant proof that God loves us and loves to see us happy.
—Benjamin Franklin, 1779, in a letter to Andre Morellet

The time-honored maxim "You are what you eat [or drink]" is true. That's why I've developed a substantial muffin top (formerly known as love handles). With every passing day I crave sweets more. I don't know whether it's because my body is making a last-ditch effort to regain former energy or whether I know my days are numbered and I subconsciously don't care if I die lumpy. Certainly I'm no longer in the dating game or marriage market, so I'm not trying to impress the opposite sex with svelteness. I rationalize with "My old body needs some fat to fall back on" (or should I more honestly say, "...to jiggle back into"?).

A coeval told me how she inadvertently caught an image of herself in the mirror as she was bending over and was appalled at how her jowls hung loose from her face. Recently, my tummy jiggled when I bent slightly over the bathroom sink while brushing my teeth. I can imagine my friend chortling, "Now you're one of us."

One of the many reasons my body is going downhill is my general dislike of milk. This distaste harks back to my childhood. At lunch when I was in the first grade I regurgitated my milk in front of a legion of peers. I had just finished eating a biscuit and had washed it down with a carton of milk. Up spewed both the biscuit and the milk. Ever since that humiliating day, I've harbored an aversion to milk. Even understanding the dietary importance of calcium and vitamin D as a twice pregnant woman, I tolerated milk only with chocolate cake and Toll House cookies. (I did, however, dutifully and lovingly serve my children milk on a regular basis. To this day, my forty-something son picks up two cartons of milk when he goes through a cafeteria line. Unlike his intractable mother, he relishes the taste of milk.)

I rue the fact that in the past I didn't adequately partake of milk. I realize too late that I might have prevented osteoporosis. Now I daily consume calcium and vitamin D enriched candies; monthly I pop a Boniva tablet. Millions of women follow this routine. (Innumerable men whose bones weaken should too.) I do have other options at this point, of course. I could undergo the fun of a yearly transfusion of a bone strengthener, or I could expose my skin to a minimum of fifteen minutes of sunlight each day, increasing my wrinkles ten fold.

As we age, it's hard to change decades-old eating patterns. When my two children were toddlers, at about the same time (they were only 19 months apart), I would devour a romance novel along with lunch while they napped. I relished this calorie-packed repast. It was my escape. I routinely ate two Dagwood sandwiches for lunch to give me strength to run after my constantly moving tots. There's no question I weighed too much for my height, but miraculously I never became rotund. Perhaps that's the reason I didn't begin to seriously worry about my food consumption until after both my children left home for college. Then I, the empty nester no longer running after my offspring and no longer regularly cooking big meals for the family, knew the time had come to rely on salads—forevermore. I broadcasted plaintively to my family and friends, "There's no way I can be satisfied with just a salad for a meal." Finally though, after a lot of years, I've trained myself to be content at mealtime with a handful of puny raw greens, fortified of course with anything else I can think of! Dousing this "rabbit food" with a tiny measure of bleu cheese dressing serves as solace. Truthfully, a salad does not comprise my every meal, but I do resort to them frequently.

Certain kinds of foods become infinitely more difficult to digest as we grow older, such as cheese, beans, raw green peppers, and broccoli. We either avoid those foods or isolate ourselves for the rest of the day from our fellow humans. For many of us, learning which foods we need to stay away from takes a lot of time, even years, and much trial and error. If we've lost our sense of smell, we and those around us are in really big trouble. For instance, in one unforgettable afternoon bridge session, I unknowingly elected to sit down at a table with an olfactory challenged old coot. He looked nice enough. However, he must've eaten something for lunch he shouldn't have. It didn't take long until his inaudible, but potently fragrant, miasma engulfed not only our foursome but others at adjacent tables. He was oblivious while the rest of us, with great politeness and restraint, struggled to breathe. This went on intermittently all afternoon.

For some of us old fogies, no food is digestible or palatable. My father, in his independent living facility which furnished three squares a day, complained incessantly and vociferously about the food. Here was a man who, before retirement, had traveled in his work and was used to being promptly and solicitously served at restaurants. He ordered whatever he was in the mood for. Waitresses (where he dined, waiters were rare), as they were referred to then, catered to his wishes. If his pork chop was overdone, they would promptly bring him a more acceptable one. When he was not on the road, my mother, an excellent cook, prepared delicious meals for him. She pampered him with his favorite dishes of fried chicken, gravy and biscuits, baked sweet potatoes, fried squash, green beans, and a variety of homemade cakes.

This superb service, the home cooked meals, and the familiar cuisine came to an abrupt halt after my mom died and Dad subsequently moved into a studio retirement apartment. In terms of food, nothing was ever done to please him, or at least, not to his way of thinking. He complained that blood traces on a chicken bone meant that the meat was either frozen too long or not cooked well enough. He refused to eat any "newfangled" foods such as pomegranates, hummus, or pita bread. God forbid someone place sushi on his plate. He unequivocally rejected fresh lettuce or anything else green, leafy, and raw, swearing they all bore e-coli. In his mind, his stash of Little Debbie oatmeal cakes staved off starvation. But Dad maintained a healthy weight until his death, which, incidentally, was due to heart failure, not food poisoning or malnutrition.

To the end, Dad avoided liquor too. It was probably just as well since the independent living rules forbade any alcohol save in a person's private quarters. Besides, solitary drinking may turn into a bad habit. But after a certain age, some of us cheerfully adopt a devil-may-care attitude. What difference does it make if we drink too much, eat too much, or smoke too much; if one evil doesn't do us in, another will. My jovial brother-in-law enjoyed his Canadian Club literally until the day he died, although mixing his pain pills with booze likely precipitated his death from a heart attack at 68 years of age. A former avid golfer, he was immobile without his walker in his last years. Still he lived to the fullest, imbibing, telling jokes and belly laughing all the way.

A lovely, tri-lingual, treasured friend in her 80s, and one of the most intelligent, literate persons I have ever had the pleasure to know, continues to drink her red wine and smoke her cigarettes. She scarfs down chocolate but eats little or nothing else. Emaciated, she's been diagnosed with lung cancer. Still she smokes! Her oncologist doesn't fuss at her either. She's persevering in her optimistic, merry way, full of projects.

I've always envied the drinking capacity of the fictional detective Nick Charles in Dashiell Hammett's *The Thin Man* (1934). In *The Thin Man* movie series, Nick, modeled somewhat after Hammett himself, consumed cocktails throughout the day, every day, and managed to retain exceptional mental acuity as well as physical stamina. Of course with Nick we're talking fantasy, but how I would enjoy that resilience!

Some of us old folks no longer imbibe because alcohol has become too toxic to justify. Another quite intelligent, beautiful friend of mine, who formerly without impairment could kill a bottle of wine in one social sitting, no longer drinks, period. Alcohol at this point in life makes her nauseous and brings on horrific headaches. Despite the fact that alcohol doesn't really agree with me anymore either, I still often drink a glass of wine with dinner. A "little glass of wine," which one of my favorite musicians, Jesse Winchester, sings about so poignantly, is comforting psychologically; it's a touch of civility in our rather uncouth culture these days. Besides, it's supposed to be good for the digestion and loaded with antioxidants (so are chocolate and coffee!).

A cocktail before dinner used to provide me enough energy to finish chores well into the evening. Now liquor sedates me so effectively I can hardly move, let alone get any work done. Any kind of spirits innervate me physically, and, I feel more tired than usual the morning after. The buzz part is nice of course. On the other hand, alcohol probably destroys what few brain cells I have left.

God help me if I ever take up pot-smoking. (Well, maybe a little THC after any necessary radiation treatment would be fine.)

Chapter Seven

Club Sandwich Generation

They'll never care about you cause you're old and in the way.
—David Grisman, 1973

My beloved daughter jokingly refers to me as "old and in the way," mainly because she's familiar with Jerry Garcia and his varied music groups. She's the only one, with the possible exception of my husband and son, from whom I'd tolerate that kind of teasing. I have to confess that sometimes I certainly feel old and in the way. Most of the time, though, I'm well aware that I'm very much needed, including by my daughter. She often needs me to baby-sit my grandsons.

Do you recall the term "sandwich generation," describing middle-age people caught between caring for elderly parents and for growing children? The concept must now be broadened to incorporate the "club sandwich generation" in which the near elderly tend a very old parent (or parents), grown children, and grandchildren. In other words, the next-to-the-oldest family member provides some kind of assistance to the oldest, the middle, and the youngest generations. In the 21st century, four surviving generations are not uncommon. The sandwich is more layered, more complex than previously. It's not unusual for us senior citizens (younger people too) to shoulder the added responsibility of physically unwell or dysfunctional siblings: those dying of cancer or some other malady, alcoholics, schizophrenics, ne'er-do-wells, those who serve jail time, and so forth. *C'est la vie* these days.

Although some early middle-aged children remain in one way or another incredibly dependent upon their parents, most people's grown children, thank goodness, are emotionally, physically, and financially equipped to take care of themselves. Likewise, as one might expect, many of our senior parents not only live relatively independently, but some continue to retain a zest for life. I'm thinking of one of my best friends whose father, into his 90s, was fond of gambling in Atlantic City. Her kind-hearted husband would cart her father to casinos to play the odds at a slot machine or some other game of chance. This classy, elderly southern gentleman was romantically pursued by old women; what's more, he played a mean game of bridge.

An impressive number of people in their 80s and 90s, some even hovering around their centennial mark, play contract and duplicate bridge. They often possess card skills far superior to that of many young players. I've significantly improved my own game by playing bridge with some of these venerable card aces.

Wish everything was fun and games. At the "club sandwich age," we experience other challenging phenomena besides helping multiple family generations. For example, many of us face the necessity of frequent visits to the doctor for various and sundry physical ailments. I resent expending time and energy with doctors' appointments; I could have much more fun hiking or reading. Add to that the frustration of no definitive answer to one's ails. Must everything be attributed to old age? I don't think so. Where are all the excellent diagnosticians such as Dr. House on television?! I suppose that as long as many of the workings of the human body remain mystifying, medicine will continue to be as much an art as a science.

I certainly dread the thought of any surgery. I don't want to go under the knife. While the majority of physicians strictly abide by the Hippocratic Oath, some surgeons are a little over-zealous. "Why wait when you can operate?" "If in doubt, cut it out." I readily admit that there's a time and place for surgery, for example, in cases of the "big C." For those of us who live long enough, the chances of developing breast or prostate cancer are high; we may have no option but to undergo surgery.

Hospital stays are not what they used to be. Contracting a lethal staph infection such as MRSA is a pervasive risk now, especially for the aged. And where have all the Registered Nurses gone? Seems one's care is increasingly in the hands of practical nurses and nurses' aides, talented though they may be. And, of course, a sojourn in the hospital can bankrupt a person. Gray panthers, unite! We have nothing to lose but our wholly unsatisfactory health care system.

Yet another both physical and cultural challenge in old age is that of "invisibility." Our status reminds me of the "Cellophane" character in the Broadway and movie hit, *Chicago*, who laments: "you look right through me, walk right by me...." One of my dearest friends is a truly beautiful woman, sought by photographers to model for ads or features in local publications. She's in her mid-70s, her hair naturally snow-white, her figure trim. When I complimented her one day on her striking good looks, she "humphed" and then responded, "Janice, no one looks twice at a woman with white hair."

On the *Today Show* recently, their "resident" medical doctor hosted a segment, including call-ins and emails from viewers, on the issue of insomnia. At no time in the discourse were the elderly mentioned. It's common knowledge that we seniors wrestle with sleep problems. Is there not a critical enough number of us in the viewing audience of that particular show to justify our incorporation in their agenda? Perhaps not, although our general elderly population adds up to millions and is growing. Are our sleep aberrations too insignificant to address in this kind of public forum? Is there an assumption that insomnia comes with age so there's nothing that can be done about it, that we have the luxury of sleeping in or taking naps, or that we'll soon sleep forever anyway so that we should just "chill out" (pun intended)?

Do you hate it when anyone younger than sixty patronizes you? I don't mind a person holding the door open for me when my arms are full or offering to assist me in picking up a heavy object. What I abhor is the latent attitude of superiority and condescension in statements such as "Oh, isn't she darling?!" It's analogous to the adult perception of babies or very young children as helpless, mindless, harmless miniatures. In such situations I burn to deliver a smart-ass commentary.

Another television program I happened to catch (while eating lunch alone at home and filling my husband's role of channel-flipper) included a scene of blatant patronizing of an old person. The show was a re-run of *Matlock*, one of the original lawyer-detective series. Of all things, that ancient codger himself, Andy Griffith, and his lawyer daughter on that episode stared dismayingly at their only witness to a crime—an elderly woman. Their smug expressions spoke volumes as to the infirmness, vulnerability, innocuousness, senility, and hence, unreliability they assumed. Surely the (younger) directors of the show were to blame for this little piece of condescension because, I promise, Andy Griffith in his esteemed character appeared as wrinkled and gray as the old crone. What irony.

A quite different irritant but still a noteworthy one for me in my club sandwich age is the lack of a decent dance partner. I continue to dance fairly well even though I realize that if I boogey too hard and long, I'll pay a price for days after, sometimes weeks. (As a friend confirms, it's not a question of *if* I'll hurt at my age, it's a question of *what* will hurt and for how long.) I can't count on my husband as a partner because he would rather chew linoleum than dance. Besides, he can hardly walk, let alone dance. Given that the majority of men don't dance or don't dance well (I'm sorry, men, but this is true—perhaps testosterone and dancing ability are incompatible. No, seriously, it has more to do with our culture than anything else, but I'm not going to delve into that sociological treatise here), there's usually always a shortage of male partners no matter what age.

My biggest problem with partners is the old male chauvinist, the one who can't dance worth a darn, yet attaches himself to me like glue. He does this because either a) he prides himself that he can still "cut a rug," b) he's lonely, c) he finds me a contemporary who's not too bad looking for her age, or d) he can't imagine that any poor old woman wouldn't love his male companionship, so much so that she can't escape, even across the room, without his hot pursuit. I sympathize only with b).

Unless they're requested to do so, younger men don't ordinarily choose senior women as dance partners. In their place I wouldn't either, what with all the gorgeous young honeys available.

Chapter Eight

Avoid Stepping in the Fountain of Youth

> We old folks are a rich demographic, ripe to be mined by the producers of a wide range of products—anti-aging ointments, virility-enhancing pills, and products too personal to discuss but that are nonetheless advertised on the evening news.
> —from "Advice for making friends and keeping friends—don't use the 'O' word" by Susan Trulove

William F. Buckley, Jr., years ago in a television interview commented about his health something like this: "I'm doing well for someone who is disintegrating." That's perhaps the best way to generally describe us senior citizens. Physically, most of us are not what we used to be, right? Stand perfectly upright immediately after having sat in a chair for awhile? No can do. Not me anyway. My doctor recently informed me that I suffer from degenerative bone disease. Swell. I'm now on a Boniva regimen, but so far, I sure as heck don't move as gingerly as Sally Fields.

That's not my only problem. Take my bladder, please! (Henny Youngman, a famous vaudeville comedian, is turning over in his grave.) Both my husband and I are plagued with urinary frequency. As our shared primary physician quips sadistically, "You're at that age." At night, half blind, he and I each totter multiple times to the bathroom. One of my darling friends expresses the same phenomenon this way: "My husband and I are like two ships *pissing* in the night."

My bladder is a poor excuse for an organ. Thank goodness for super absorbent panty liners (I prefer not to wear adult waterproof underpants because the plastic makes me sweat). I've been wondering how I'm going to manage my urinating in the yard when Mikey and I move to our downsized house. Yes, you read me correctly. I said urinating. You see, when I tackle yard work, I usually don't like to quit once I've started, so I don't go into the house when I feel the urge. Besides, my sneakers are too muddy. If I don't heed the urge when it initially nudges, I'm in trouble. Outside in the yard I skedaddle to the nearest cover. In our present sizeable, very private backyard, I can run behind the bushes and trees, pull down my tattered jeans and squat before I wet my pants. At our future domicile, however, there will be no place to hide out of neighbors' view. The yards in the new hood all closely abut. What's more, some fellow infirm people may reside there who have nothing better to do than to watch me pee.

Another kind of excrement has become a problem for me: flatulence has evolved with a vengeance. For someone whose boyfriend once exasperatingly accused her, "You act like you're too good to defecate," it's most embarrassing to be plagued with flatus. (I need to add that "defecate" wasn't the actual word the boyfriend used.) And hemorrhoids—bah, humbug. I treat them medicinally but still they persist. I have irrevocably entered the epoch of corporeal crudity, not to mention pain.

I've strutted and fretted my hour upon the stage until strutting has become too physically demanding to continue. In the past, my professional success required at least a modicum of nice appearance. As a college professor, I had to stand before classrooms of students, faculty members at various and sundry meetings, parents when they came to visit, community gatherings, and the college board of trustees at times. Having retired years ago, I at least no longer have to fret over my image in the workplace.

I do, nonetheless, feel compelled to favorably impress my precious grandchildren, even if it's with disclaimers. At one juncture I found it necessary to explain to my 4-year-old grandson that there are certain things I cannot do, such as jumping on his pogo stick or foot racing, because of my old body. Further I told him, "Your body is new so you can do just about anything you want to." After having enlightened him on this particular difference between him and me (yes, this is the correct pronoun usage so don't sneer; you're just not used to correct grammar), he is fond of reminding me, sometimes in public, "O'ma, you're old and I'm new."

Remember the time-worn joke about the senior citizen who woke up one morning without pain so she thought surely she was dead? *C'est moi.* I clearly recall as a child being bored silly by elderly people who sat around and lamented about nothing but their aches and pains, not to mention death. I call it the pastime of "You tell me your pains, I'll tell you mine." Now I'm old and must chide myself when I start whining about my physical and mental state. So O.K., I'm repentant for what follows.

Mama really did tell me there'd be days like this. She advised me not to panic or worry, though. She said as she grew older she endured various and sundry aches and pains, describing them thusly: one week she'd feel a new pain which would go away sooner or later, and then she'd withstand another pain somewhere else in her body which would also disappear as mysteriously as it had arisen. As usual, she was right. I've encountered some disturbing and, thank goodness, passing physical maladies. For instance, several years ago on occasion, a sharp pain lasting 1 or 2 seconds shot through my head. The excruciating pain caused me to grimace involuntarily. I experienced this several times a month for many months. The bad news is that some dilapidated blood vessels probably blew in my brain. The good news is two-fold: I obviously don't need those vessels because my gray matter remains intact (well, sort of), and I haven't experienced anything like that since. Knock on wood.

Without pain or undue difficulty I used to dance, swim, hike, and do yard work. Although I persevere in most of those activities, it's not easy. Yard work has always served as a real catharsis for me, and I suppose because of my Appalachian Scotch-Irish heritage, nowhere else do I feel closer to the Almighty than when I'm digging in the dirt. And as my husband describes me, I'm queer for flowers. I still take great pleasure in puttering around in the yard, but I can't shovel, tote gallons of water, or heave a mattock the way I used to.

In bygone days I went out in the snow, even shoveled a small walkway once in a while. Now I dare not venture out in the snow, and most certainly not in ice, for fear of falling. Thus I've avoided so far the misfortune which befell my husband last Christmas morning. We awoke to a seasonal and bewitching covering of snow. We had planned on driving very early in the morning to my daughter's house to watch our two grandchildren gleefully dive into their Santa Claus surprises. I took one look at what appeared to be black ice on our brick stoop and patio out back and announced to Mikey, "I'm not leaving this house." My dear husband, always the adventurous and optimistic soul, said, "I think I'll just step out the back door and see for myself." "Bam!" he instantaneously slid, catching himself on his knees. I gasped, then cried as I helplessly watched him try to move. The brick surface was so slick, he literally had to crawl back inside the house. We never made it to my daughter's house that day and despite repeated medical treatments, Mikey has limped ever since. Note that my husband's tumble wasn't caused by infirmity. Falling is not by any means a monopoly of seniors, but it's usually much more difficult to recover as we advance in age.

A certified klutz, I've taken spills all my life; as a doddering oldster I've had my share of falls too. In hindsight, my more recent topples seem down-right slapstick. One of my offbeat mishaps occurred on Election Day 2008, when Barack Obama was chosen President. In my ecstasy over the election results I bought red, white and blue balloons enough to post a tri-colored, vibrant patriotic display in my front yard as well as in those of my two grown children, who also celebrated Obama's victory. Election time occurs, of course, in the fall when the leaves form a profusion of color on the trees as well as a profusion of leaf piles on the ground. One of those piles of leaves hid the protruding corners of some slate walking stones in my front yard. As I "tripped the light fantastic" decorating with the balloons, I also tripped over one of those stone corners, cursing my reckless abandon as I fell, full-body, panic-stricken, irrevocably into leaves and hard ground beneath. Never wearing one of those help gadgets around my neck, I lay there for several minutes (seemed liked hours), not one neighbor in sight, before I could move. With great difficulty, I dragged myself into the house and called Mikey at work. As usual, he hurried to my rescue, waiting for hours with me in ER. To mend my fractured ankle bone, I hobbled around for weeks wearing one of those over-sized, clumsy, ugly black boots on one foot.

Perhaps the most farcical fall I've taken can be blamed on a puddle of urine. My 4-year-old grandson was spending the night with me—a common, most pleasurable custom with my two grandchildren. I dutifully made sure he urinated before he climbed into bed where we carried out another common, most pleasurable custom, that of reading a couple of children's books as he drifted off. As soon as he was fast asleep, I groggily made my way to my own bed, just across the room from him. Inexplicably, about an hour-and-a-half later I heard my darling boy sobbing his little heart out. With only the nightlight shedding any illumination, I bolted out of bed. "Honey, what's wrong?" I anxiously called out. No answer.

As I neared him, his back to me, little quaking body hovered against the back of the small sofa bed with his head down on folded arms, I discovered the calamity. In fact, I stepped in it. Not only stepped in it, but slid in his innocent puddle of urine on the floor. The telephone from the nightstand clattered to the floor as I attempted to grab onto something, anything to break my fall. Alas, I hit the wood floor face first. With an inordinate pain on the side of my face, I slithered my way over to my grandson, cleaned him up and replaced his soaked pajama bottom with dry clothes, then guided him safely onto my dry bed. Seriously aching and sleepy, I left his wet sheets until morning. I did manage to grope my way in the dark to the kitchen downstairs where I assembled a makeshift ice pack to alleviate the throbbing facial pain. With ice pack in tow, I hurried back upstairs to make sure my little prince was O.K. I needn't have worried; he didn't stir 'til morning. The next day I suffered minor contusions and a nasty headache from another silly fall. My grandson recalled only a nightmare of a big bug biting him.

Ah—the fountain of youth! Avoid stepping in it.

Chapter Nine

The Funeral File

> I bequeath myself to the dirt to grow from the grass I love,
> If you want me again look for me under your boot-soles.
> You will hardly know who I am or what I mean,
> But I shall be good health to you nevertheless,
> And filter and fibre your blood.
> Failing to fetch me at first keep encouraged,
> Missing me one place search another,
> I stop somewhere waiting for you.
> —Walt Whitman, "Song of Myself," verse 52

This is a second chapter you mustn't feel compelled to read. Oh, it's interesting. But for the most part, I've learned it's better for me not to contemplate obliteration; you may think the same way. As I mentioned at the beginning of this book, over my lifetime I've spent too many precious hours worrying about death. A second reason for my caveat about skipping this chapter if you wish is because each of us has to come to terms with mortality in his or her own way. What has eased my mind might not ease yours. What I've learned late in life may be old hat to you. Suit yourself.

Have you started a funeral file? If this sounds morbid to you, rethink. I'd never heard of such a thing until some close women friends of mine mentioned they began a funeral file years ago. They convinced me it is a good idea, so now I've compiled one. It contains my written wishes to be cremated and to have a festive wake in lieu of a somber funeral. At the wake I'd like people to sing with gusto, recite moving poetry, drink lots of wine, and celebrate life. To make it easier for my family to implement my requests, I've stuffed the file with some of my favorite quotations, poems, and instructions on where to find music I love.

Mortality is closing in on me as I realize I was born when FDR was still kicking (well, maybe not kicking but hand paddling in Warm Springs, GA); that I can remember Truman leaving the office of President to the tune of "Poor Little Robin, walkin', walkin' to Missouri;" and that I have witnessed the presidency of a peanut farmer, two notorious womanizers, a movie star, and a man "of color" (hallelujah!). This is not to mention living to see the women Condoleezza Rice, Nancy Pelosi, and Hillary Clinton overcome gender barriers to secure exalted political appointments. I hope now to survive long enough to celebrate a woman president....

The recent dying off of numerous of my favorite old movie idols is another factor in bringing home my impermanence. (The old rock stars seem to keep going, however, like the Energizer Bunny. Mick Jagger, Neil Diamond, and Paul McCartney, for example, just keep right on rockin' and rollin'.) Actors and cinema always loom large in the psyche of us moviegoers. The first film star death that struck me hard was that of Rock Hudson. What a hunk. My premiere sexual dream as an early adolescent featured Rock Hudson; in fact, I dreamed about him at least 4 nights in a row after I had seen the movie *Giant*. When I learned of his sexual proclivities, I was bereft for us women. Then when I learned he was dying from AIDS I was terribly saddened to think that he, or anybody else for that matter, should die in such a gruesome manner.

None of us knows when or how we'll meet our demise; we just know it's gonna' happen. Through the years I've been fortunate to have had sagacious acquaintances who've given me invaluable perspectives on death. One was a female psychiatrist about 70 years of age. When I talked with her about my fear of death, she responded that she didn't lose any sleep over it. She said in her infinite wisdom, "Janice, I wear death like a cloak." In other words, she knew the Grim Reaper was hovering, but she accepted his presence as an integral part of her humanness, not as a threat. Another person whose perspective alleviated some of my mortality angst was one of my grad school professors. His was no doubt a very old, unoriginal idea, but it was one I had not encountered until then. As a group of us academics loitered in the halls of ivy one afternoon waxing philosophically, the discussion turned to death. My professor said, "A person is not cognizant either of a pre-life or a post-life. All a person can know is the here and now, so make the most of it. Don't worry about what comes after; you'll never know while you're still alive." George Santayana offers similar counsel: "There is no cure for birth and death save to enjoy the interval." The renowned conservationist John Muir remarked that we come out of eternity, and upon death, we go back into eternity.

My son Jay, who is approaching middle-age, takes the scientific approach. He tells me, "Mom, every living thing has to die and that is good. Death is necessary for new life." Still a youngster back in 1985, he composed the following:

> All creation destroys,
> All destruction creates.
> In order to truly
> appreciate life,
> One must witness death
> and celebrate.

When facing death, those who possess steadfast religious faith should derive immense comfort. They're the fortunate ones. Ever-questioning, I'm inclined to skepticism. Because I'm professionally trained as an empiricist, it's difficult for me to subscribe to the unseen and the unknown, or to operate purely on faith. I do, however, derive solace knowing that when I die, my strewn ashes will nourish nature's awe-inspiring beauty and miraculous physical glory.

We each have our own way of the Welsh poet Dylan Thomas's raging "against the dying of the light." Many years ago when my husband was at his mother's house for lunch, he noticed that she washed the dishes in shadow; there was no light over her sink. A devoted son, Mike purchased several easy-to-install florescent tube lights to put up over her sink the next time he dropped in. After he installed the lights for her, she asked, "What do I do when the lights burn out?" Mikey responded, "Just throw them away; they're disposable. But don't worry, those lights are good for at least 2000 hours; they will outlast you by a long shot." At first his mother appeared delighted with her new lighting, but apparently she later brooded about Mikey's comment on fluorescent longevity. The next time he came back for lunch, there she was again, washing the dishes in shadow. He questioned her, "Why don't you turn on the lights I installed for you?" She snapped back, "I'm saving on their life-time. I'm determined to be here as long as they are!"

A married couple who have been friends of ours for decades banter playfully that each wants to be the first to leave this earth. Neither wants to tackle the horrendous task of unloading all the household furnishings and knickknacks they've accumulated over the years.

I'm fully appreciative of having survived this far, and in good health. I've seen many family members, friends, celebrities and role models die before me. When we reach our senior years, we may feel that our life span is incredibly short, but a century ago in the U.S. a person typically lived only 50 years or less. Today in a developing country, such as some of those in Africa, on average a person lives only 45 years.

Those of us in technologically advanced nations may linger too long in life, facing formidable philosophical, financial, or physical issues. I prescribe a carpe diem attitude along with heavy doses of humor. Entering my seventh decade, I've adopted a daily morning mantra: I say to myself, "Something wonderful is going to happen today." And you know what? Be it ever so humble, it usually does. My husband takes me to lunch at my favorite deli, my son brings his adorable female schnauzer over to romp with ours, my daughter invites me to a chick flick, or my grandson's tongue twisters make me laugh until tears roll down my cheeks.

My dear, jovial brother-in-law, now deceased, used to tease me often with "Just relax, Janice; you're never going to get out of here alive." He might just as well have said, "Be happy, don't worry," right? I used to think both these adages trite. Now I realize their profundity. (Apropos, my sister granted my brother-in-law's request to play Sinatra's "My Way" at his funeral.)

Some techno geeks predict that within the 21st century, death as we know it will disappear. For instance, a few die-hard computer futurists envision human brains being kept alive indefinitely within the body of a robot. English biologist Aubrey de Grey views the aging process as a disease which can be cured or halted. These ideas may strike you as insanely far-fetched, totally ludicrous, or even undesirable. Nonetheless, recently with the enzyme telomerase, Harvard Medical School researchers were able to reverse the aging process in mice suffering from physical degeneration. Although scientists and futurists subscribe to widely varying perspectives as to just how long and in what way the human life span will be extended, it's fair to say that both groups are optimistic about increased longevity.

So you younger folks, take heart. You may live forever!! Or at least much longer than previous generations—and in much better mental and physical condition.

Chapter Ten

I Don't Know the Difference between Goldfish Food and a Puppy

...Macavity's a Mystery Cat: he's called the Hidden Paw—
For he's the master criminal who can defy the Law.
He's the bafflement of Scotland Yard, the Flying Squad's despair:
For when they reach the scene of the crime—Macavity's not there!
—T.S. Eliot. *Old Possum's Book of Practical Cats,* 1939

Eliot created charming, whimsical names for his feline characters. We fancied them so much that we chose two of them as a double name for one of our schnauzers. Despite her non-cat status, as well as her gender, we dubbed our schnauzer Jennyanydots Macavity.

We've adored all four of our schnauzers, our preferred breed because they don't shed (our little boy suffered from allergies). Each one has brought immeasurable joy and love to our lives throughout the years. One of our treasured doggies is still with us, but he's on the last of his four legs.

An often heard quip among seniors is, "You aren't truly retired until the children are grown and the old dog is dead." As far as 21st century North American children are concerned, the platitude should more accurately assert "after the children have left home for good." Currently, grown children return home at alarming rates! As to the dog part, flippancy rather offends me when it pertains to my faithful canine friends. To my fellow dog lovers, I don't have to gush about how wonderful they are or what great companionship and unconditional devotion they provide. Perhaps you own cats, or as cat people attest, your cats own you. Whichever the case, I'm sure you view them as irreplaceable.

By the time we reach advanced age, if fate has smiled upon us, we've nurtured a number of pets. And we've also endured the passing of more than one of them. Such gladness and enrichment they bring us, then such deep sorrow when we lose them. Their deaths can be as heartbreaking to us as the loss of a cherished human being. The demise of a loyal, devoted, four-legged pet sometimes merits more tears than that of a human.

In our latter decades we grieve at the loss of more and more persons as well as pets. My husband said never again did he want one of our doggies brought home to our backyard for burial because I'm such an emotional wreck during the process. Mikey feels very uncomfortable around a profusely sobbing female. Truth be known, he hurts deeply too. To show how tender-hearted he is, he's had made for each of my deceased puppies a small stone plaque with their name and dates. Those plaques rest side by side in my favorite flower garden.

So what's the better choice for me: a flood of tears at home or holding a meager, limp body in a back room at the vets, futilely attempting to grieve discretely? After the vet gently takes the doggie from my arms, I try to escape through the waiting room as fast as possible, red-eyed, shoulders racked with uncontrollable blubbering. The other pet owners sitting, waiting to see the doctor, involuntarily stare at my contorted visage.

Last year, when my third precious schnauzer died, I had her cremated. I intend to spread her ashes around the verdant, undisturbed edges of our backyard. For the moment, I'm content with holding on to the small tin box containing her dust. Hey, at least I didn't have her body stuffed and mounted over my fireplace as one of my zealous friends threatened to do with her deceased miniature poodle.

I sorely miss the unique qualities of each of our three deceased doggies. We have a photograph in a family scrapbook showing our first schnauzer puppy, Max, and our toddler nephew both peeing at the same time in our backyard. We joke that the two were toilet trained together. Our females, Jennyanydots and Himey, intuited my feelings to an amazing degree; I thought of each as my canine soul sister. Jekyll, the last of our doggies, still dashing but not quite as vigorously, is our "talker." He constantly tries to tell us something with his barks. We don't always understand his communication, but we appreciate his efforts.

I refer to our dogs as serial schnauzers because after we became owners of our first one, we acquired three more in succession as each died or significantly aged. We picked up our first schnauzer from a pet store when my young daughter (at the time) and I went out to buy goldfish food. We just happened to be watching the antics of the puppies for sale when we irrevocably fell in love with the runt of a litter. In our nurturing weakness, we brought the scrawny, furry little bundle home with us. When we arrived, my husband's first comment was, "Don't you two know the difference between goldfish food and a puppy?!"

Retired but still living in their own home, my mother- and father-in-law were both crazy over their little white poodle, Jacques, a gift to them from their daughter. At first my mother-in-law, Adah, was wary about having a dog again and so late in life. She felt she had already experienced that dubious pleasure when her children were growing up. My father-in-law, Bob, maintained a stern facade with his family members, including pets. Soon, however, both Adah and Bob doted on the miniature, hyperactive creature. Jacques served as both Adah's watchdog and her ears. If it were not for him alerting her with his bark, she would've missed anyone lurking around outside or on a brighter note, many a welcome knock at her door. Every evening in the living room Jacques would stand watch on the back of the wingback chair placed at the window and await Bob's arrival from the golf course. Ordinarily the grump, Bob grinned widely when Jacques bounced off the chair, danced on his hind feet, and greeted him with excited yips. My father-in-law fondly kept the poodle's curly hair immaculately groomed, brushed his teeth, and sprayed breath freshener into his pet's mouth. Bob contended that his actions were purely practical. Of course, he didn't want any of us to think he had become sappy in his old age.

One has to admit, though, that as well as bringing happiness into their lives, dogs can present a hazard for the elderly. Inadvertently tripping us seniors qualifies as one of the most prevalent, and sometimes comical, dog-induced problems. One summer day just a few years ago I was walking across my front yard, gardening tools in one hand, full gallon watering can in the other. I thought my two schnauzers were leisurely trailing behind me until one of them accidentally but forcibly clipped me from behind at the knees, sending my legs flying out from under me. I think he spotted a squirrel and made a dash for it. Fortunately I didn't suffer too much damage; I landed on the grass on my fat-padded derriere. Other older folks are not so lucky in their dog run-ins.

These days, with Jekyll following close to my heels, I walk very carefully up and down my steps or through the house. Dogs (and human toddlers, I might add) have been known to cause a fall when underfoot and out of sight of a person carrying a loaded laundry basket.

I have to confess too that I'm tired of picking up dog poop. It never ceases to amaze me how even small dogs can produce so much *merde* (Google this French profanity if you can't guess the meaning). Greatly sparing my arthritic back, my daughter gave me one of those little rake and shovel sets designed for cleaning up after dogs. I don't have to bend over so much as I'm canvassing the yard, clearing it of pet droppings.

It's not really my dog who is troublesome, though. It's me. I'm the old curmudgeon. At this stage in life I'm physically and mentally weary of taking care of everything: rambunctious critters of any kind, dysfunctional relatives, the house, the yard, the car, clothes, my body, houseplants, you name it. If it needs tending, I pass.

Now that I have that whining off my chest, I have to own up to the truth that I'll probably eventually get another dog after Jekyll's demise (which we fervently hope is not any time soon). Nevertheless, we're not planning to look right away for the boon companionship of another dog. Until we quit traveling altogether, pet care is too problematic for us. My only genuine regret concerning dogs and cats is, as every SPCA calendar photo reminds us, that there's not enough time to savor the myriad of awesome breeds.

If I spend my waning days in a nursing home, I hope my family will help me find one that allows pets. Many retirement facilities now welcome the presence of pets, dogs being one of the favorites. Studies show that a dog or cat can greatly enhance the well-being of an elderly person. Four-footed friends can entertain, assuage loneliness, decrease blood pressure, ward off depression, and make us get up and move around. Walk the dog—it's not just for yoyos anymore.[1]

NOTE

1. Whether or not you could perform "walking the dog" back in the '50s, it remains a staple trick among yoyo champions.

Chapter Eleven

Retired and Outrageous

> Old age is an excellent time for outrage. My goal is to say or do at least one outrageous thing every day.
> —Maggie Kuhn, founder of Gray Panthers

In our advanced years we can be outrageous for good or for bad. I'll never forget witnessing two old married people yelling nastily to each other at an airport. Perhaps they were both deaf and had to yell to be heard. All the old clichés and jokes are true when it comes to trying to communicate with an elderly, deaf person. Quadruple the frustration when communicating with an elderly, deaf, not-fond-of-communicating-in-the-first-place husband. Top that with "is it his deafness or is he just not listening?" We're all familiar with the old "tune her out" tactic. I should retort to my husband sometimes with one of his own favorite utterances: "Do I have to tattoo what I just said on your derriere?"

Did the unpleasant airport couple gradually fall into a marital script of hateful come-backs? We know that marriage is often a power game. Sometimes the wife is dominant, but for my generation, it's more common for the husband, as the major wage earner, to impose his will. When the husband retires, he may expect to continue to rule the castle. But not my dear husband. I think he's lost hope for that expectation.

Many males don't know what to do with themselves when they retire, especially if they are no longer physically able to participate in sports. My husband regularly gripes that God has shrunken his golfing ability but not his stomach. If men harbor any feelings of emptiness, restlessness or uselessness, they're not apt to talk about it. They're disinclined to go to the doctor to see what ails them. Too many men do not maintain close ties with family members besides their wives. Traditionally it's the latter who most often nurtures relationships with family as well as friends; she visits, writes the notes, shops for gifts, throws the parties, sends the emails and makes the phone calls. We're all familiar with these older male tendencies. Lacking medical attention, social connections and a sense of purpose, too many men die soon after they retire.

Men, I want to share this newsflash—you might live years longer if you take up housework—seriously! One of the reasons that women outlive men is because the majority of females don't ever retire, at least in terms of household chores. Most women, until totally disabled and regardless of occupation outside the home, continue to do housework.

Even though my husband does a lot of baking, washing dishes, social networking, and even babysitting the grandchildren (if he is required only to literally sit), he undertakes precious little housecleaning. Before Mikey and I were married, he informed me that he didn't do toilets. In my younger days I was such a submissive, repressed, stereotypical good little woman that I didn't call him on that declaration. My bust. Forty-three years later he's still not doing toilets. Okay, I'm sympathetic with the reluctance on anybody's part to clean privies or even to vacuum and dust. I especially balk at moving dust; it rates up there with mowing grass as a waste of valuable human energy. But unless one is affluent and can afford hired help, housecleaning falls to each of us. If you don't want to wallow in the squalor, somebody has to do it.

After approximately 30 years of marriage, I informed my husband that I was retiring from cooking on a daily basis. Turn about is fair play: he no toilet, me no cook. I grew tired of all those hours spent planning, shopping for, and preparing meals. I reprise the role of chef for occasional dinner parties, holidays, our women's bridge foursome, or whenever I'm in the mood. Otherwise, Mikey doesn't hold his breath on waiting to be fed.

As an aside on generational differences, I'm amused and not just a little envious of many younger married women these days who inform their husbands, even before marriage, that they don't cook. You go, girl! On the downside, though, I worry about the health of children from a union where neither mommy nor daddy cooks. If you've been raised on junk food or even a diet of granola bars, dried fruit, and drinks from a plastic pouch, physical robustness may be difficult to attain.

Getting back to the old couple at the airport, their hostility towards each other could stem from a variety of factors: having been married for what seems like forever, irritability from ill health, or some ancient grievance. Maybe the wife nurses anger even after a half century or more, because while she stayed home and took care of their babies 24/7 (which I venture to say applies to innumerable mothers of my generation), her husband watched TV and played golf. Perhaps they just get on each other's last nerve. We old married folks can certainly get on each other's nerves (and everybody else's). My husband has crushed my feelings more than once when he has said to me, "I always love you; it's just at times I don't like you." I finally appreciate where he's coming from with that statement. Now in my dotage, all I have to say is, "Right back at ya', Dude."

I told Mikey years ago, I think right after the scene I observed at the airport, that I refuse to squander my last years in a quarrelsome, hateful marital relationship. Those seniors seeking divorce after 50, 60 years of marriage apparently share my view. I want to grow old in the sweetest ways possible, to bask in love and peace, man, like the closet hippy I remain. Though Mikey and I haven't yet attained nirvana, we're improving. As we canter towards the sunset, we old cowpokes are working on our cordiality towards each other.

Not only do most of us have to adjust our marital relationships as we age, but also we have to adapt to retirement from our jobs and careers. Retirement is especially challenging for those of us who grew up steeped in the Protestant work ethic. We have to learn how to relax or play. We can't identify with "take this job and shove it;" instead, our motto is "anything worth doing is worth doing well." We constantly set goals, suffer guilt when we're sick in bed, and feel uneasy "burnin' daylight." We don't like leaving off until tomorrow what we can do today.

I come by these values naturally. My father epitomized the Protestant work ethic. After dutifully serving overseas in WWII, he came home and managed a lumber company. Then with the lure of a much higher salary and greater benefits, he left the lumber business and began his grueling, thankless career of long distance, trailer-truck driving. At 55 he retired from professional driving and took on the job of supervising public school custodians. He retired after a decade of that hassle. The last job he held was night watchman at an ITT plant. He stayed there until he turned 75, when he was physically unable to continue. A multiple retiree, Dad was glad for the jobs and glad for the pensions. At the independent living facility where he resided until his death at age 91, he readily assumed the responsibility every night of locking the second floor entrance. As always, he was diligent on his watch. Both he and the administrators of the facility were pleased with his usefulness. Until macular degeneration rendered him almost blind, he was in charge of the funds and of booking bands for a bi-weekly senior dance at a local recreation center. He was an extremely dependable, trustworthy, capable man.

In his work ethic, my dad mimicked his dynamo mother. She raised four children, labored tirelessly on the family farm, sold her produce, and helped run a catering business. After her husband died, she remained on their farm until the day she climbed a tree to pick apples and fell and broke her hip. She was in her early 80s. At that point, her sons had to place her in a nursing home. But that didn't mean she ceased to labor. She voluntarily carried out the task of filling the water pitcher in each room of the nursing home where she resided until her death at age 99. The staff at the home happily accommodated her desire to be useful.

Unlike many, my dad and grandmother found satisfying occupations throughout their lives. Experiencing a fulfilling retirement can pose difficulties. If one is a true professional, one's entire identity rests on his or her life's work. Giving up that self is hard. But many of us have acquired valued wisdom and know-how in our respective fields which can transfer to another niche in the "golden years." For instance, my 80-something cherished *amie*, retired professor of French, conducts a "Salon" at her home every Sunday afternoon. Under Professor Lynn's tutorage, participants cheerfully sip wine and practice their French (they're not allowed to speak any other language during salon hours). Lynn also serves as a lively, devoted, extremely knowledgeable docent at our local art museum. Her energy and enthusiasm in pursuing a wide array of activities and interests puts the rest of us to shame.

Barring any severe mental or physical impairments, those of us old timers living into the 21st century can engage in a variety of enjoyable, and certainly constructive, activities in retirement. Assuming satisfactory health, adequate financial reserves, and the desire, we can travel, near or far. We can take more time to nurture relationships. We can reserve computer time at our local public library. Even if we're not physically mobile, we can access Internet, Netflix, Nook, and Kindle from our homes! An added bonus: we can nap when we want to. My dear retired chemistry professor buddy, age 90, describes consciousness as an awkward interlude between naps. With a little imagination, courage, experimentation, or perhaps altruism, retirement can be the best time of our lives. What the heck! Now is the time to have fun. We've earned it.

Having spurred you with tempus fugit, carpe diem, and all that jazz, I'll tell you what your parents always told you, "Do as I say, not as I do!" Given my heritage, it's challenging for me not to work all the time. I've progressed about as far as a busman's holiday— I'm still engaging in historical research, my former professional occupation. Can somebody save me?!

Chapter Twelve

New Tricks

With age comes wisdom, but sometimes age comes alone.
—Oscar Wilde

We "near" elderly and "already there" elderly are encouraged to keep our mental faculties sharp by learning something new and challenging. (If we suffer from Alzheimer's, we may not have that option; science reveals that little at this point can ward off that dreaded disease.) Conscientious, self-disciplined individual that I've always been (perhaps it would be more honest to say the masochistic, obsessive-compulsive person that I've always been), I am dutifully striving in my old age to undertake challenges. Right on.

One of my utmost endeavors past the age of 65 is trying to learn to play the piano. After three years, my keyboard mastery comes nowhere close to Liberace's (unless you're a senior, you may not know of this flamboyant, t.v. superstar pianist of the late 1950s) nor to Sir Elton John's who just turned 60 and is touring with his band. For starters, try tickling those ivories with arthritic fingers. Second, I'm having a heck of a time memorizing the letter locations of bass clef notes. Luckily I learned to read treble clef in elementary school (long ago, in a galaxy far away), so reading the top line of a musical score comes fairly easy. Problem now is I get confused between the bass and the treble notes.

One of the most precious gifts I've been granted is having a renowned professional as a piano teacher. I was able to connect with Liz only because she is a resident musician and music professor at the college from which I retired. She agreed to give me lessons out of the kindness (or was it pity?) of her expansive heart. How much longer her patient mentoring will last, I dare not think. She recently assigned me a waltz by Mozart which so far I've managed only to massacre. That disgusting little genius Mozart composed the piece when he was five years old! What an affront to my venerable age.

Hey, if Beethoven in total deafness could play the pianoforte and compose the Ninth Symphony, I should be able to play Chopsticks with a little arthritis in the hands and a somewhat defunct brain, right?

One of my other inspired moves in attempting to recharge the gray cells was taking a refresher computer course at our local community college with my 40-year-old daughter, Jamie. I had earlier contemplated such a course with one of my female buddies, but that fell through for me. When Jamie suggested that we take a computer course together, I enthusiastically seized the opportunity. I knew I would enjoy hanging out with her, and since computer programs seem to advance daily, I was eager for the technological update. What did I have to lose—or so I thought. My children discovered years ago that their parents have clay feet, but with this episode, I think my daughter actually wanted to disown me.

Unlike my son and daughter, my expertise with computers is limited to word processing, search engines, and email. Even with email I'm delinquent, though. I read somewhere once that according to computer etiquette (another oxymoron given what boorish garbage appears on-line), it's rude not to answer an email within 24 hours. To the great annoyance of some of my friends who live by their Blackberries and/or who've worked at a computer most of their professional lives, I don't check my email for a week, even two. I'm an old-fashioned, ornery, antiquated cuss who resists the "virtual" life. I keep a hardcopy date book. I prefer face-to-face or real voice-to-voice communication. I do not Tweet, YouTube, or Facebook. I safeguard my privacy as much as possible in our George Orwellian world. I don't send e-greeting cards. I don't keep a budget, consult my bank account, and rarely shop on-line. I've had little experience with spreadsheets and I'm definitely inept when it comes to the latest data bank programs such as Access.

When their parents deem my grandchildren old enough to text, I'm sure I'll finally attempt texting. By then, it may be the only way to keep in touch with them. We all know how busy teenagers become and how some of them communicate almost exclusively through texting.

Unlike me, my husband considers his computer a godsend. Since my son years ago introduced him to the PC, he's been addicted. Mikey happily whiles away the hours working and playing at his computer; I gladly defer to him for highway maps, movie schedules, vacation plans and so on and so on.

To try to catch up with my skilled family and the rest of the world, I signed up for a computer course with my daughter. The instructor, a wisp of a child, was a computer wizard. She spoke in an exasperatingly soft voice and conducted her class at a terrifyingly fast clip for an old timer like me. Our computer manual was huge, with a minimum of 500 pages, and the instructor covered it all. I wore my hearing aids in class, but when she spoke too whispery or with her back to us or from the back of the classroom, I couldn't decipher her words. Since I didn't want to be a complete pest in class, I would ask Miss Wisp only occasionally to repeat what she had said. Instead, I frequently turned to my daughter with, "What'd she say?" Given the pace of our instruction, Jamie too missed what our teacher had said.

On top of these impediments to my learning (Jamie's also), most of the students in the class whizzed right along with the instructor.

They worked full-time with computers already and were taking the course to upgrade their skills and/or their positions and salaries. The oldest person in the class, I was not only old and cold but old and slow. How to compete under these circumstances?

Jamie became increasingly irritated with me sitting beside her in class. We had to share the computer manual because it was too expensive to purchase a copy for each of us. She often needed to refer to the manual at the same time I did but on a different page—not the most advantageous arrangement. I persisted in asking her to repeat information I couldn't hear and to show me how to do one thing or another on the computer. In my panic when I missed a lightning-fast detail from the teacher, under my breath I blurted out "Shit!" (my choice but rare expletive). It's not really clear to me whether Jamie chuckled at my outbursts or was mortified. When we did our assignments or took our exams in class—they were always on-line—she invariably had to sit around and wait for me to finish. She was not happy to waste her valuable time. (She keeps to a very busy schedule what with raising her two boys, keeping house, gourmet cooking, working at her community theater, tutoring for pay, etc., etc.) When the class finally ended, I said to her, "Well, at least I enjoyed getting to spend special time with you." She hesitated for a second too long and responded with something like, "This 'special' time together was not under the best circumstances." Translation: "You've got to be kidding me!" I sensed then, as I had throughout the computer course, that my technological denseness as well as my slowness, deafness, willfulness and general obnoxiousness tried her patience. I don't blame her.

Regardless of the outcome of that course, I admire computer geeks such as Miss Wisp. I don't use the word "geek" in a derogatory sense; after all, I'm a geek too, just not a computer one. Also, it doesn't make sense to be overly envious of a computer whiz. Most of us could excel in a chosen field if we dedicated all our time and energy to it. I dare say computer geeks typically spend most waking moments perfecting their skills.

In any case, computers have transformed our modern world. Not too many years ago my daughter and I, on a more level playing field in this instance, were proud and happy to receive our respective certificates of merit for attending a one-day seminar in auto repair. Well, forget the instruction of that day. Try manual repair or even trouble-shooting under the hood of a late model car. Everything is computerized. And forget changing a tire by yourself now—lugs are embedded nearly humanly irretrievable with air hammers. I've witnessed a large man standing with his full weight on a lug wrench who couldn't budge a lug.

One has to be a true Renaissance person just to function on a day-to-day basis now. I'm not too impressed with the accounts of U.S. frontier days which depict men and women as remarkably self-sufficient, hard-working, talented, bold, and innovative. Please. As far as I'm concerned, compared with modern-day expectations of the average person, those pioneers led a life of leisure. Let's take a few examples of the early American wife's chores: how complex were housekeeping and child-rearing for her? She basically swept one dirt floor in her small log cabin. Because she didn't have access to a great variety of foodstuffs, a big pot of goulash hanging over a fire sufficed for dinner. She laundered very few clothes because the family possessed scarcely any. And she never had to chauffeur the kids because children participated in precious few activities besides work around the homestead. Besides, given the types of transportation and educational opportunities available in the early 19th century, where and how far could the pioneer kiddies go?

Sure, Laura Ingalls, aka Melissa Gilbert, on *Little House on the Prairie* gets around a lot, but that show definitely aggrandizes backwoods life. As Paul Lynde once answered on *Hollywood*

Squares to the question, "What's 100 times sweeter than sugar?"—"Little House on the Prairie."

On *Little House*, Laura's frontier mom escaped the intricacies of 21st century life. The modern woman must take a significant amount of time in wielding at least one complicated vacuum cleaning machine over far larger square footage. She needs to learn not only the nutritional value of, but to cook expertly on sophisticated stoves, all manner of exotic foods. Food shopping and meal planning require big blocks of her time. To do laundry, she must wisely separate huge piles of clothes and linens by color, fabric, and label instructions and then dial the appropriate setting on the most environmentally-friendly, complex washer and dryer possible, making sure to use the right detergent (or non-detergent), bleach, fabric softener and dryer sheets. It takes forever to put all the clean laundry back in the proper places. If any of her "labor saving" devices should break, she must call a repair expert, for an expensive fee, before she can resume her particular task. Of course, getting in touch with such a repair person usually entails a minimum half day for locating the manual that came with a machine, searching that same manual for the 800 number to call, listening and responding carefully so she can push the correct number on the phone the first time around, and if she's very lucky, finally being given a local number she can call for assistance. The repair person may be able to come to her house next week.

The contemporary mother transports her offspring from one place to another all day long, year-round—playschool, pre-school, school, place of worship, music lessons, art lessons, dance lessons, swim lessons, multiple sports camps, summer camp, computer camp, doctor, dentist, orthodontist, allergist, child psychologist, speech therapist, birthday parties—you name it, there she goes. Heaven forbid in addition to running her household, Mom has to work outside the home to afford the appliances and camps.

I feel compelled to add that even for many so-called children's toys these days, it takes a genius Mom or Dad (or grandparents) to assemble them, let alone to help little ones learn how to play with them. For example, my grandsons' clever and loving parents spent days last Christmas helping them erect a huge Lego pirate set. With hundreds of tiny pieces, the kit included every conceivable object associated with pirating: daunting ships, skiffs, villainous swashbucklers, swords, knives, canons, treasures, skull and crossbones flags, etc.

Not only are my body and mind obsolete, but I'm dizzy with our increasingly perplexing households, not to mention our incredibly fast-moving, digital, robotic, ever-expanding outside world.

Epilogue

And Now You Want to Know if There Is Anything Good to Say about Getting Older

…We aren't as judgmental as we used to be.
We're quicker to laugh, and not as eager to blame.
There's time left in this game. May we find
(Along with the inability to tell ourselves that we'll keep playing forever)
A few compensations….
—Judith Viorst. *Forever Fifty and Other Negotiations*. New York: Simon and Schuster, 1989

Discussing the pace of life with a friend, I remarked how busy I am in my advanced age. Trying to commiserate with me she said, "Oh, it was like that for me for the first few years after my retirement," as if I'd get over it. Ha! It's going on seven years since I retired and the full schedule has not abated. In fact, I'm still crossing off things on my bucket list. I might like to tutor high school students in history, sociology, or whatever (eons ago, before I returned to graduate school, I substituted a month for a high school advanced math teacher and enjoyed it). In this day and age, I could use a Spanish course. I dream about spending a couple of leisurely weeks in Tuscany or in the Lake District in England. I want to introduce my grandsons to Western Europe. Ah, so many delightful things to do and learn, with so little time.

Through it all, love abides. When I'm away for an extended period my preschooler grandson, unprompted, tells his mom, "I miss O'ma." When I arrive home from my sojourns, my little schnauzer jumps up and down with pure joy. Although pleased, husband Mikey exhibits a bit less exuberance upon my return.

This Valentine's Day my Mikey sent me a big box of candy wrapped in red cellophane. But that's not all. In a slit in the red cellophane he had inserted a package of hearing aid batteries—that's true love, folks.

In my very blessed universe we senior women and men treasure our families and friends. We enjoy our homes, we work, travel, golf, play bridge, and dine out. Some of us even tweet and have joined the hordes on Facebook and MySpace. We exercise, read, learn new things, go to the movies, and on occasion, throw parties. We dance as if no one is watching.

In (most of) our endeavors, in good health or decline, in economic prosperity or distress, friends and family provide support groups. How can I not feel upbeat when my husband smoozes me (some more of my daughter's "now-speak") with, "Don't you look pretty?" "Compared to what?" you may ask; or, he says, "You're the prettiest woman in the room." "What room?" you may ask. Who cares. Everything's relative, including age, finances, physical condition and love.

All in all, the senior years are a lovely and rewarding time of life. For some of us, the best.